BRUCE TEGNER'S
COMPLETE BOOK OF
JUJITSU

THOR PUBLISHING COMPANY
VENTURA CALIFORNIA 93002

Library of Congress Cataloging in Publication Data

Tegner, Bruce.
    Bruce Tegner's Complete book of jujitsu

    1. Jiu-jitsu.   I Title   II. Title:
Complete book of jujitsu.
GV1114.T434   1977   796.8'15   77-5023
ISBN 0-87407-516-5
ISBN 0-87407-027-9 pbk.

First edition: October 1977
Second printing: August 1977
Third printing: May 1982
Fourth printing: September 1984

The author wishes to express his gratitude to
MIKIO KATSUDA and LARRY REYNOSA
for demonstrating the techniques. The work
of Linda O'Neill and Barbara Phillips is much
appreciated.

BRUCE TEGNER'S COMPLETE BOOK OF JUJITSU

**THOR PUBLISHING COMPANY   P. O. BOX 1782
VENTURA   CA   93002**

Printed in the United States of America.

BRUCE TEGNER BOOKS REVIEWED

SELF-DEFENSE: A BASIC COURSE
"An eminently practical, concise guide to self-defense...for young men not versed in the martial arts...step-by-step instructions...keyed to action photos...in logical progression...
American Library Association BOOKLIST

"YA - A calm, nonsexist approach to simple yet effective self-defense techniques accompanied by clear photographs and sound advice." SCHOOL LIBRARY JOURNAL

BRUCE TEGNER'S COMPLETE BOOK OF JUJITSU
"...authoritative and easy-to-follow text..."
SCHOOL LIBRARY JOURNAL

BRUCE TEGNER'S COMPLETE BOOK OF SELF-DEFENSE
Recommended for Y.A. in the American Library Association
BOOKLIST

BRUCE TEGNER'S COMPLETE BOOK OF JUDO
"...the definitive text...ideal for instructors and individuals."
SCHOLASTIC COACH

SELF-DEFENSE & ASSAULT PREVENTION FOR GIRLS & WOMEN (with Alice McGrath)
"...should be required reading for all girls and women..."
WILSON LIBRARY BULLETIN
"...simple and straightforward with no condescension...easy to learn and viable as defense tactics..." SCHOOL LIBRARY JOURNAL

SELF-DEFENSE FOR YOUR CHILD (with Alice McGrath)
[For elementary school age boys & girls]
"...informative, readable book for family use..."
CHRISTIAN HOME & SCHOOL

DEFENSE TACTICS FOR LAW ENFORCEMENT
"...by Bruce Tegner, a noted authority in the field...would be an excellent textbook for a basic course in self-defense..."
LAW BOOKS IN REVIEW
"...a practical tool for police academy programs, police programs at the university level, and for the (individual) officer..."
THE POLICE CHIEF

SELF-DEFENSE NERVE CENTERS & PRESSURE POINTS
"...a practical guide to the most effective weaponless self-defense using the least possible force...(and)lowest-risk-of-injury body targets. ...Students...and teachers of self-defense and sport skills will find much valuable source material in this book."
THE POLICE CHIEF

KUNG FU & TAI CHI: Chinese Karate and Classical Exercise
"...recommended for physical fitness collections."
LIBRARY JOURNAL

SOLO FORMS of Karate, Tai Chi, Aikido & Kung Fu (with Alice McGrath)
"...well-coordinated, step-by-step instructions...carefully captioned photos...for personal enjoyment and exercise... useful for individual or instructor..." YA
American Library Association BOOKLIST

CONTENTS

CONTENTS

THE MARTIAL ARTS

As it is used today, the term "martial arts" covers a wide range of activities derived from ancient Asian styles of hand-to-hand combat. It would be logical to include European and American styles of boxing, wrestling, fencing and archery among the martial arts; they, too, are derived from ancient battle skills. But in current usage, only the Asian fighting forms comprise the martial arts.

There is considerable dispute about the origins and history of the martial arts. There are records of similar fighting methods being practiced in other countries from at least 2000 B.C., but the specifically Asian styles are thought to have come to China by way of India and Tibet. From China, knowledge of various forms of weaponless fighting spread to the other Asian regions. Although Japan may have been the last of the Asian countries to acquire the martial arts, with the exception of Chinese kung fu karate, it is the Japanese forms which are most popular and most widely practiced in the Western world.

A great many diverse fighting systems which developed in Japan are known by the term jujitsu.* Among the jujitsu systems there are dozens of main styles; if substyles are taken into account, there are literally hundreds of different kinds of jujitsu. It is not accurate to refer to any one as the authentic or official style; there is no standard form of jujitsu.

Stylistic differences are present in all forms of the martial arts and their European equivalents. Stylistic differences may be so subtle that they are apparent only to those who have experience in the field, or they may be substantive. Observation of the activity and comparison with a variant form are the only ways to acquire reliable information about style.

---

*Until recently there was no standard English spelling. A common form was "jiu jitsu," which I used in earlier works. Others used "ju jitsu" or "jujitsu." *Roget's International Thesaurus* uses "jujitsu." In 1975 the *Encyclopedia Americana* adopted the spelling "jujitsu" and that is the form which will be used in this book.

JUJITSU & JUDO

In the 1880's Dr. Jigaro Kano, a Japanese educator and sport enthusiast, introduced a new style of jujitsu. Dr. Kano had studied and classified many of the ancient jujitsu methods and had selected techniques from among several styles. He called the synthesis judo. Dr. Kano's new jujitsu had two distinct forms. One form was comprised of throwing and grappling techniques. This form has evolved into the modern sport we now know as judo. Judo is recognized and practiced as a sport throughout the world, and is an official Olympic Games event.

The other part of Dr. Kano's judo consisted of hitting and kicking techniques combined with holds and locks for restraint. Although Dr. Kano clearly distinguished between judo for sport and judo for self-defense it was confusing to use a single term to describe two different activities. The part of Dr. Kano's judo which he called self-defense judo has again come to be called jujitsu.

A form of sport jujitsu was introduced after sport judo became popular in Japan, but it was never widely adopted. Early in the twentieth century jujitsu contest matches were held in Germany. The Germans used weight classes in jujitsu matches, which greatly amused the Japanese, who were convinced that size was not a significant factor in jujitsu or judo. When the AAU and Olympic Games judo committee modified the rules of judo to include weight classes, players were matched by weight and through preliminary elimination meets. The Japanese custom was to match contestants by belt rank only, but since belt ranking was not a standardized procedure, contestants were often mismatched in weight and skill.

Dr. Kano is shown opposite, photo 4, observing practice at his school, the Kodokan. The players wear the judo gi (gee, with the "g" as in "go") now commonly worn for jujitsu practice. In earlier times jujitsu was practiced in the hakama (hah kah mah), a uniform presently associated with kendo and aikido (photos 1-3).

1

2

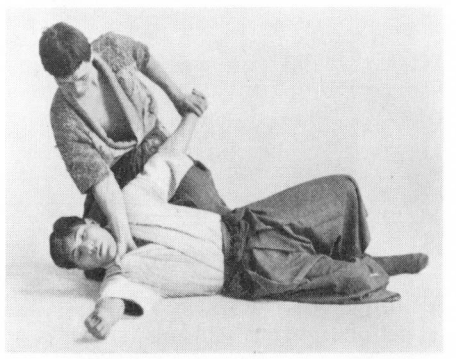

3

4

 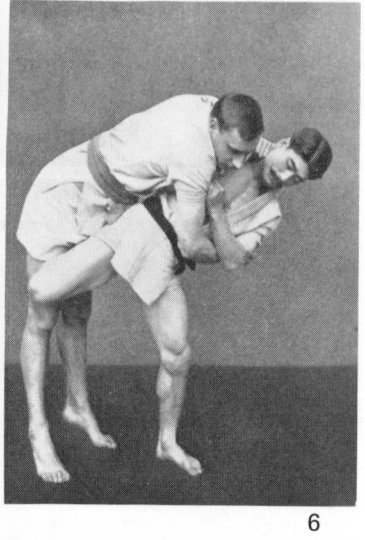

5   6

After the hakama was discarded and before the judo gi
was adopted, jujitsu was sometimes practiced barelegged
in a short-sleeved jacket.

COMPARING FIGHTING SYSTEMS

Although there are a great many names for different
styles of fighting systems, there is a relatively small group
of basic techniques used in all of them. No matter what it
is called, a hand-to-hand fighting method will employ
one or more of the basic techniques shown on the chart,
opposite.

No other system of the martial arts uses as great a
variety of techniques from among all the categories as do
the jujitsu methods. Within the classification of "jujitsu"
there is considerable variation in emphasis and style. One
system of jujitsu might emphasize kicking and throwing
techniques; another, throwing and grappling. Some styles
of jujitsu emphasized hitting and kicking to such a degree
that they are indistinguishable from what we know today
as karate. Today's kenpo karate was previously known

	AIKIDO	BOXING	JUDO	JUJITSU	KARATE & KUNG FU	SAVATE	WRESTLING
Fist blows, blocks & parries		●		●	●	●	
Open hand & arm blows				●	●	●	
High kicks				●	●	●	
Low kicks				●		●	
Holds, locks & grappling	●		●	●			●
Throws			●	●			
Takedowns	●		●	●	●		●
Nerve centers & pressure points emphasized				●	●		
Training emphasizes flexible response rather than rigid, prearranged actions		●				●	●

as kenpo jujitsu. Some styles of jujitsu used techniques from all of the categories, weaponless as well as crafted-stick and cutting weapons, and found weapons such as farm implements -- the flail, for example.

7

8

In books intended for the Western reader, jujitsu experts often wore street clothes. Katas were rarely demonstrated; jujitsu tricks were stressed.

WAZAS & KATAS

Jujitsu of any style is characteristically taught as a series of specific movements. First the student practices a specific attack/defense action, using a single technique. This is called a waza, sometimes rendered into English as "trick." After the separate tricks or wazas are practiced singly, they are combined into series of attack-counter-takedown-and-hold actions which comprise the kata, or routine. The kata is still in the process of evolving from a combat training activity.

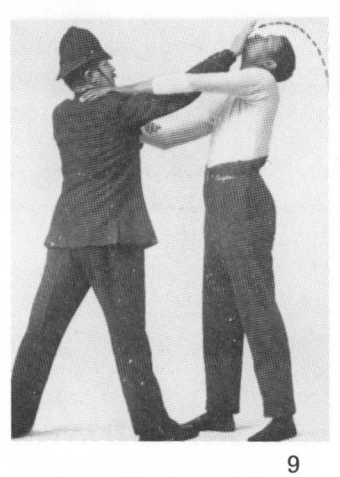
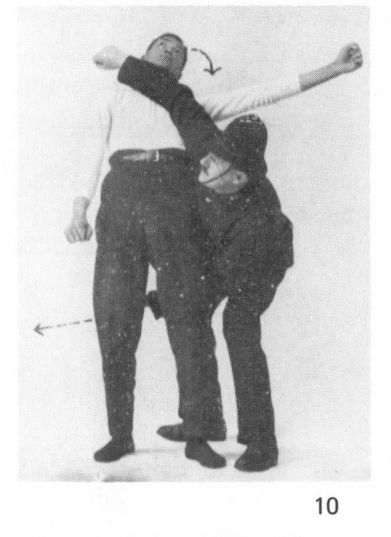

9   10

Police use of jujitsu was advocated in many Western countries and taught in some of them.

Because the wazas and katas are prearranged and learned as specific responses of defense to a specific action of assault, a great many katas must be learned if the student is to acquire enough skill to be able to use jujitsu as self-defense. And because they are complex and difficult to learn, the student of jujitsu is expected to spend years in training and practice in order to achieve a suitable level of skill. This is one of the reasons why, in my view, jujitsu in its old forms is not appropriate for practical self-defense today. Another drawback is that most jujitsu methods used the greatest force possible against any assault, reflecting an era when personal vengeance was permitted or overlooked.

The katas in this book have been selected from a number of old-style jujitsu methods. A few of the old katas (the kneeling and sword katas) have been included as examples of the ancient routines. Much of the material has been modified to provide an activity that is appropriate for recreation, health and fitness, eye-hand-body coordination and self-improvement through physical self-expression.

JUJITSU & PRACTICAL SELF—DEFENSE

For self-defense my preference is a considerably modified form of jujitsu* which employs a relatively small number of techniques which can be used in a flexible way against a great number of possible assaults; which can be used by smaller individuals against larger assailants; which does not require constant, ongoing training; which does not treat every instance of assault as though it were a vicious attack. Finally, I question the practicality and necessity of learning every defence with a restraint technique. Only law enforcement and security personnel are required to restrain and hold an assailant or suspect; the lay citizen has no such responsibility. It is more prudent, sensible and safe to consider escape from a threatened assault as the preferred choice. If physical defense is unavoidable, it is best to use only as much force as will stop the intended assault and allow the intended victim to escape.

I make these distinctions between jujitsu and my concept of practical self-defense because there are still many misconceptions about appropriate applications of the martial arts. The same factors which mitigate against jujitsu as a modern-day self-defense make jujitsu a splendid, interesting and exciting activity for other purposes. The student who has learned practical self-defense and who wants to continue a related physical activity will find the perfect solution in jujitsu. Those individuals who enjoy learning the techniques of the martial arts but who do not have an aptitude for nor an interest in sport competition will find jujitsu practice an excellent alternative. The very difficulty and complexity of the jujitsu katas offer challenge and a rewarding experience to those who enjoy learning body skills.

Law enforcement groups can practice jujitsu for practical as well as health and fitness benefits. Perfecting the restraining techniques <u>does</u> require constant, ongoing practice; performance of jujitsu katas is a pleasant and useful way to maintain the skill needed in the field.

*Tegner, Bruce. 1975. <u>Bruce Tegner's Complete Book of Self-Defense</u>. Ventura: Thor Publishing Company.

11

12

13

Arm lever techniques were favorites among teachers of
jujitsu for self-defense. The takedowns shown in photos
10, 11 and 15 are variations of an arm lever with back trip.

14   15

16

WOMEN & JUJITSU

During feudal times, women would not have been included in jujitsu training. From the time when Dr. Kano introduced his form of jujitsu women participated in the practice of the sport but were not encouraged to participate in judo contests. In books intended for Western readers from the end of the last century to the middle of the twentieth century, women have been shown practicing jujitsu. Although the katas in this book are demonstrated by men, there is no reason why women cannot practice the material illustrated.

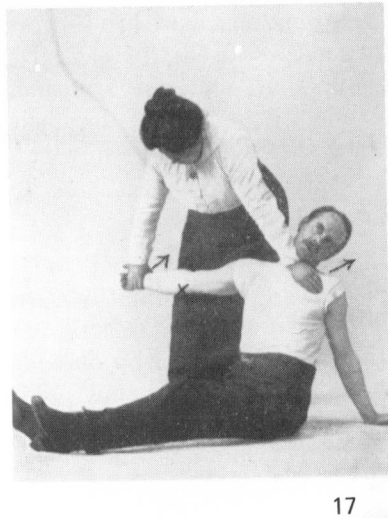

17   18

In photo 18 the aggres-
sor (shown left) repre-
sents a Western-style box-
er.   The choke hold in
photo 19 is seen in sport
judo today.

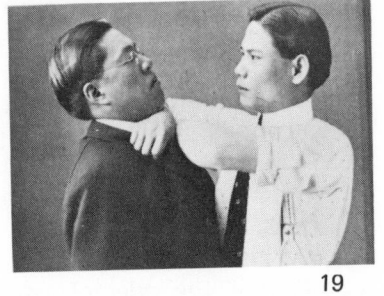

19

COLORED BELT RANKS

Contrary to widespread belief, the first black belt holders
were not deadly killers; they were skilled sportsmen.
The combat forms of the martial arts did not award proficiency ratings graded by belt color. Belt ranks were
introduced in judo, the first of the martial arts to be
modified and adapted for modern sport and physical
development. When the sport form of judo was introduced, judo players were ranked according to skill in
competition and ability in demonstration of formal
techniques.

The martial arts which were considered purely as self-
defense, that is, having no sport form, did not award
colored belt degrees until long after they had been used
in judo. In some systems of kung fu (gung fu) one

might hear a term such as "five year man" used to suggest rank, but no outward mark of rank was used. Increasingly, the martial arts, including jujitsu systems, are awarding belt ranks. There is no standard scheme or color; belt ranks are significant only in the school or system in which they are awarded.

TORI & UKE

The Japanese words tori and uke will be used in this text. TORI (toh ree) is the man who demonstrates the action in the single techniques. In the katas it is he who defends against the attack and applies the takedown and hold. UKE (oo keh) is the passive partner in the demonstration of single techniques. In the katas, he simulates the attack, but does not resist or counter tori's responses.

Because the katas are prearranged and rehearsed and there is no resistance offered, the partner who performs tori's actions can concentrate fully on technique. He can give complete attention to practicing well-balanced, smooth flowing body movements and graceful gestures.

SAFETY in PRACTICE

In any kind of body contact activity, accidents are likely to occur if the rules of safety are not observed. When partners share a concern for safety and health and when they follow the rules of safety and the cautionary notes which are found in the text, the possibility of accidental injury is at a minimum. OBSERVE THE SAFETY PRECAUTIONS. DON'T FOOL AROUND.

It is more important to learn the gesture and movements in any technique than it is to develop speed. A technique which is learned correctly can be speeded up with practice. Working slowly, you can concentrate on technical perfection and body movement. Working slowly is a good learning procedure and it is a good safety procedure.

The techniques which are inherently dangerous, such as eye-gouging and windpipe chokes, have been eliminated from this presentation of jujitsu. The hand and foot blows which are included must be practiced without contact.

HOLDS & LOCKS

To learn and practice the basic movements of the holds and locks, students take turns as tori and uke. Tori repeats the action of each hold until he can perform it smoothly, gracefully and correctly. Uke is a passive partner; he does not resist the application of the hold, nor does he assist tori by anticipating tori's action.

There is no need for rough practice procedures. Safety can be ensured and the possibility of accidents can be minimized by careful observance of some simple rules:

From the first day of practice, students should know and use the tapping signal for release. Uke taps twice to tell tori to release or stop the action. Tapping is a more practical signal than a verbal command because it can be used when talking would be difficult (as in a choke hold). If uke can tap with his hand, he taps tori twice, or taps himself, or taps the floor. If uke's hands are immobilized, he can tap with his foot. Uke must tap the moment he feels pain, or if a hold or lock is being applied too forcefully. Tapping twice is also the signal for submission. Tori must release instantly upon getting the tapping signal.

Beginning practice should be done in slow motion.

Students must avoid rough or snappy action in the application of holds and locks.

In practice of the choke holds, pressure is applied at the side of the neck; pressure against the windpipe is strictly forbidden.

Notes: Except where otherwise indicated in the text, tori is shown at the right in the first photo illustrating each technique. Natural and unnatural grips: If you reach forward as though to shake hands and grip in that manner, you will be using a natural grip. If you reach forward and then turn your hand over so that the thumb points downward, your grip will be unnatural.

OUTWARD WRIST LOCK

20. Tori (shown right) steps forward with his left foot as he extends his left hand to grasp uke's right hand, using an unnatural grip.

21. Tori raises uke's captured hand so that the palm is toward uke; as uke's hand is raised, tori grips it with his right hand.

22. Tori takes a deep step with his right foot, placing it next to uke's right foot and at the same time he twists uke's captured hand counterclockwise.

23. Pressure is applied by continuing the counterclockwise twist and bending the captured hand toward the wrist.

20

21

22

23

INWARD WRIST LOCK

24. Tori steps forward with his right foot as he grips uke's right hand with both his hands, his thumbs on the back of uke's hand and his fingers into the palm.

25. Maintaining his grip, tori takes a step with his left foot and begins to pivot clockwise as he raises the arm and twists the captured hand.

24   25

26. When he has completed the pivot, tori applies pressure by holding the captured arm high as he twists and bends the hand toward the wrist.

HAND LOCK

27. Tori grasps uke's right hand with both his hands, placing his thumbs into the palm of the captured hand.

28. Tori pulls the captured arm forward and raises it, palm up, applying pressure by bending the hand down as the wrist is raised.

27

28

HAND LOCK with ARM BRACE

29. Tori pivots clockwise as he grips uke's right wrist
with his left hand and uke's right hand with his right hand.
Tori's right-hand grip is like a handshake.

30. Tori raises the captured arm and turns the hand palm
up as he pulls uke forward, off balance...

31. and braces his bent left arm under uke's elbow.
Pressure is applied by lifting with his bent arm as he bends
uke's fingers back.

29

30

31

OVER–SHOULDER LOCK

32. Tori takes a step clockwise with his right foot as he grips uke's right hand with both hands; his thumbs are at the back of uke's hand and his fingers are into the palm.

33. He extends uke's arm as he turns the captured hand counterclockwise...

34. and raises it as he pivots clockwise...

35. and draws the captured arm, palm up, across his left shoulder. He applies pressure by pulling down and cross-body on the hand and arm.

32

33

34

35

THUMB HOLD

36. Tori grips uke's hand at the base of the thumb...

37. and applies pressure over, back and down.

36

37

ARM BAR & VARIATIONS

38.   Tori grips uke's left wrist with his left hand...

39.   and pulls the captured arm as he twists it counter-clockwise...

40.   and continues to twist as he steps toward uke with his right foot and presses down at uke's elbow, using the bony edge of his forearm to apply pressure. As tori presses down with his forearm, he pulls up on the captured wrist.

38

39

40

41. In this variation, tori uses his palm to apply pressure at uke's elbow.

42. In the second variation, tori uses his elbow to apply pressure at uke's captured elbow.

43. In the third variation, tori places his right hand at uke's back and with his right knee he applies pressure at uke's captured arm.

41

42

43

ARM BAR/ELBOW LOCK with LEG PRESSURE & WRIST TWIST

44. Tori (shown left) applies an arm bar at uke's right arm and uses follow-through to take him to the ground.

45. Tori steps over uke's captured arm as he grips uke's captured hand with his left hand.

46. Pressure is applied by locking uke's elbow with his left leg as he twists uke's wrist and levers it toward his left leg.

44   45

46

STRAIGHT—DOWN ARM LOCK

47. Tori steps with his left foot and grips uke's right wrist with his left hand.

48. He takes a step with his right foot as he slides his right arm under uke's captured arm...

49. and bends his right arm and applies pressure with the bony edge of his forearm against uke's upper arm as he pushes outward at uke's wrist.

47

48   49

CROSS—BODY HAND & ARM HOLD

50.   Tori steps counterclockwise to place himself at uke's side and grips uke's left wrist with his left hand.

51.   Tori raises and turns uke's captured arm and places it palm up across his upper arm; he reaches under the captured arm and grips cloth high at uke's right side, using an unnatural grip with his right hand. Tori applies pressure by levering down with his left hand. Uke's arm is positioned so that his elbow is against tori's upper arm or elbow.

50

51

HAND LOCK with JAW THRUST

52. Tori grips uke's left hand with his left hand in a handshake grip...

53. and pulls the captured hand as he pivots counter-clockwise toward uke's side and thrusts at uke's jaw with his palm, twisting uke's head; tori continues to pull the captured hand and applies pressure by bending the fingers (uke's hand is palm up) and maintaining the lever action with his right arm.

52

53

HEAD & ARM TWIST

54. Tori grips uke's left wrist with his left hand...

55. and as he steps behind uke with his right foot he draws the captured arm across his body and turns it palm up as he prepares to...

54

55

56   57

56. grip uke's chin with his right hand.

57. Pressure is applied by pulling around and back with the right hand and twisting the captured arm back and around.

UPPER ARM LOCK

58. Tori grips uke's right hand with both hands; his thumbs are into the palm of uke's hand and his fingers are at the back of the captured hand.

59. Pivoting clockwise, tori steps around...

60. placing his right foot down behind himself as he wheels uke around and pulls and clamps the captured arm under his left arm as he twists the wrist. He applies pressure by pressing in with his left elbow and pulling up on uke's wrist as he twists and bends the wrist forward.

58

59

60

BENT—ARM LEVER LOCK

61. Tori takes a step with his left foot and grasps uke's right wrist in a natural grip with his left hand...

62. and pulls the captured arm as he slashes at the bend of uke's elbow with his right hand.

63. Allowing uke's wrist to rotate in his grip, tori raises uke's hand in an outward half-circle. Tori is now holding uke's wrist in an unnatural grip, though he has not released the grip. It is the rotation within his grip which has changed the hold.

64. Tori begins to lever uke's bent arm back as he prepares to reach under the captured arm with his right hand...

65. and takes a deep step with his right foot and places his right hand onto his left hand and bends the captured arm back sharply. Pressure is applied by levering back and down.

61

62

63

64

65

HAND & ARM HOLD with HEAD PRESSURE

66. Tori (shown left) grips uke's right wrist with his right hand and turns the arm palm up and draws it across his body and he reaches under the captured arm...

67. and around with his left hand, placing it at the back of uke's head. Tori applies pressure by pulling the captured arm across his upper arm and pressing uke's head forward.

66

67

STRAIGHT—ARM LOCK

68. Tori grips uke's left wrist with his left hand and...

69. turns uke's captured hand (clockwise) palm up.

70. As he steps in with his right foot, he raises the captured arm...

68

69   70

71   72

71. and reaches over it with his right hand to grip cloth at his own chest.

72. Tori applies pressure by cinching inward with his right arm as he presses down with his left hand.

UNDER ARM PIN

73. Tori steps in and grips uke's right wrist with his left hand. He rotates the captured hand palm up...

74

75

74. and pulls the captured arm under his left armpit; he clamps it into his body and bends his left arm to place the bony edge of his forearm under uke's elbow; tori places his right hand at uke's left shoulder...

75. and applies pressure by pushing back and down with his left arm.

ELBOW, WRIST & SHOULDER LOCK

76. Tori steps toward uke with his left foot and grips cloth just above uke's right elbow as he grasps and bends uke's right hand with his left hand. Tori applies pressure by pushing up on the captured hand as he pulls down with his right hand.

77. Maintaining the pressure, tori steps clockwise as he raises uke's arm...

76   77

78. and completes a 180° turn. Now tori is applying pressure by pushing down on the bent hand and pulling in the direction of uke's wrist with his right hand; he leans forward to apply pressure to uke's shoulder.

BENT—ARM HOLD & BAR

79. Tori grips uke's right wrist with his right hand and uke's elbow with his left hand; he raises and bends the captured arm as he twists the wrist...

80. and pivots clockwise to place himself at uke's side and pulls up at the captured wrist (uke's hand is palm up) and presses forward on the elbow...

79

80

81. and then slides his left arm across uke's arm and applies pressure at the elbow with his forearm, putting uke completely off balance forward.

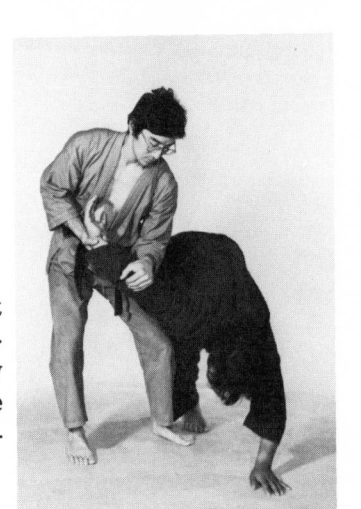

STRAIGHT—ARM RESTRAINING HOLD

82. Tori takes a step with his left foot and places his right hand at uke's left upper arm as he places the back of his left hand at uke's wrist.

83. Pivoting clockwise, tori places his right foot behind himself as he raises uke's arm by pressing with his right hand as he lifts at uke's wrist with his left arm; uke's arm slides along tori's left arm until his right wrist is locked into the side of tori's neck.

84. Tori completes a 180° turn. His left arm is across uke's elbow and his right forearm is across uke's upper arm.

85. Tori slides his right hand to the back of uke's neck; he applies pressure by pushing down with his right hand as he pulls in with his left arm.

82

83

84

85

BENT—ARM RESTRAINING HOLD

86.   Tori takes a step forward with his left foot and places his right hand at uke's right upper arm and places his left wrist at the inside of uke's wrist.

87.   Gripping and pulling forward with his right hand, and pushing back and lifting uke's arm with his left arm...

88.   tori bends uke's arm as he steps clockwise to place himself next to uke's right side; he slides his right hand forward and presses at uke's neck or head to push him down; he locks uke's captured bent arm into his body.

89.   Tori grips uke's captured wrist with his right hand and grips his own right wrist with his left hand and applies pressure by twisting his body clockwise as he presses down with his arms.

86

87

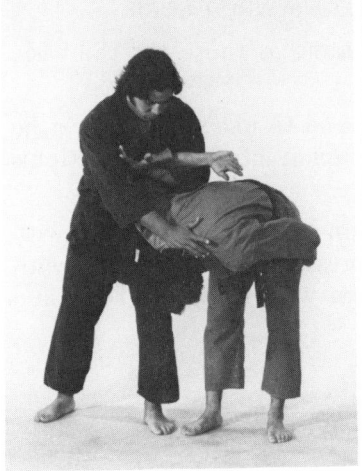

88

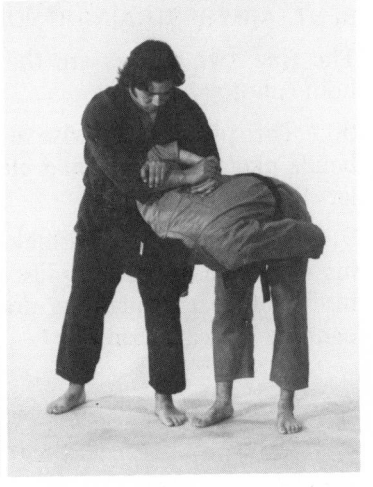

89

90   91

BENT—ARM RESTRAINING HOLD with WRIST LOCK

The first two moves are the same as those for the basic hold (photos 86-87).

90. Tori pivots clockwise around to uke's right side as he bends uke's right arm and clamps it into his body with his left forearm...

91. and applies a wrist lock on uke's captured hand with his right hand. Tori applies pressure by clamping in with his left forearm, pressing down with his upper body and bending the captured wrist.

FRONT BENT—ARM LOCK

92. Tori grips uke's right wrist with his right hand and...

93. slashes into the bend of the elbow with his left hand.

94. As he takes a step with his left foot, tori raises uke's captured arm in an inward half-circle, allowing uke's wrist to rotate in his grip. When uke's arm is raised and bent, tori slides his left hand across uke's arm and grips his own right wrist.

92

93

94

95

95. Tori takes a step with his right foot to place it behind uke's right foot and applies pressure by levering back and down.

ELBOW LEVER

96. Tori steps forward with his right foot as he grips uke's right wrist and slashes into the bend of the elbow with his left hand...

97. and steps with his left foot as he raises uke's captured arm in an inward half-circle, allowing uke's wrist to rotate in his grip. Tori places his left hand under uke's elbow...

98. and takes a step with his right foot as he levers straight over and back, pulling with his right hand and pushing with his left hand.

97   98

WRIST & ELBOW LOCK

99.   As he steps toward uke with his right foot, tori slashes into the bend of uke's right elbow with his left hand and grips the back of uke's right hand with his own right hand...

100.   and bends uke's captured hand toward the wrist as he places his left hand behind uke's elbow and presses; the simultaneous pressure with both hands is viselike.

101.   As he pivots clockwise to make a 180° turn, tori slides his left hand under uke's bent arm and places his left hand over his own right hand and clamps the captured arm firmly into his body; tori applies pressure by pulling toward himself with both hands.

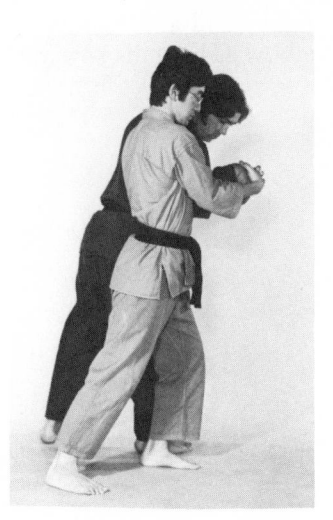

100   101

102   103

102.   In a variation of this technique, tori grips and
bends uke's hand with uke's fingers pointing upward (com-
pare this with photo 100 in which uke's fingers point
downward), grips the elbow and applies the viselike pressure...

103.   and pivots 180°, positions his left hand over his
right hand and maintains the clamping action with his left
elbow as he pulls toward himself with both hands.

REVERSE WRIST & ELBOW LOCK

104. Tori grips uke's right hand at the fingers with his right hand and places his left hand at uke's elbow...

105. and pivots clockwise as he bends uke's arm and slides his left hand between uke's arm and body...

106. and applies pressure by bending uke's wrist down (uke's hand is palm up) and pressing at the captured elbow. The action is viselike.

104

105

106

PIVOT & ARM—TWIST LOCK

107.   Tori grips uke's right wrist with both hands...

108.   and pulls the captured arm forward and out to the side as he begins a counterclockwise pivot...

109.   twisting and...

110.   raising the captured arm high...

107

108

109

110

111

112

113

111.   as he completes a 180° turn...

112.   and pulls down on the twisted arm...

113.   and pulls it up uke's back as he continues to twist the captured wrist.

114

115

BENT—ARM LEVER with PIVOT

114.   Tori grips uke's right wrist with both hands...

115.   and pulls the captured arm forward as he begins to...

116.   pivot clockwise...

116

117

118

119

117.   raising the captured arm as he turns...

118.   and begins to bend the captured arm as he completes a 180° turn.

119.   Tori leans forward slightly and applies pressure by bending and levering uke's arm downward.

BETWEEN—LEG ARM LOCK

120.   Tori steps with his right foot and grips uke's right wrist with his right hand...

121.   pulling uke forward as he steps around to uke's side.

120

121

122.   and behind him...

123.   and he thrusts uke's captured arm between uke's legs and grips the wrist with his left hand.

124.   Tori releases his right-hand grip and applies pressure by pushing at uke's back as he lifts uke's captured arm.

122

123   124

ONE—ARM CHOKE

125.   Tori reaches (palm down) and grips cloth high at uke's right shoulder; his thumb is inside the garment.

126.   He reaches under his right arm to grip cloth at uke's chest.

127.   Tori applies pressure by pulling cloth with his right hand as he levers his right forearm against the side of uke's neck and pulls cross-body with his left hand.

125

126

127

CROSSED—ARM CHOKE

128.   Tori grips cloth high at uke's left shoulder, with his left hand, his thumb inside the garment.

129.   He takes an identical grip with his right hand high at uke's right shoulder.

130.   Tori applies pressure at the sides of uke's neck by pulling toward himself with both hands as he uses a reverse-scissors action with his arms.

128

129

CAUTION: In practice, the pressure should be applied to the sides of the neck only. AVOID pressure on the windpipe.

130

131

132

CHOKE HOLD with HEADLOCK

131.   Tori steps toward uke with his right foot as he grips cloth at uke's left shoulder (close to the neck) and places his left hand behind uke's right upper arm.

132.   With a vigorous, thrusting action, tori spins uke counterclockwise as he steps clockwise...

133.   behind uke...

134.   without releasing his right-hand grip at uke's left shoulder (cloth).

135.   Tori reaches under uke's left arm with his left hand and places his left hand at the side or back of uke's head. Pressure is applied in a scissorslike action by pulling around and back with his right arm and pushing at uke's head with his left hand.

133

134

135

136   137

CHOKE HOLD with KNUCKLE PRESSURE

136.   Tori grips and twists uke as he did in the preceding choke hold with headlock (photos 131-134).

137.   Tori reaches over and then under uke's left arm and applies pressure by digging into uke's back with his knuckles as he pulls back and around with his right arm.

138   139

CHOKE HOLD with ARM PRESSURE

Tori grips and spins uke as before (photos 131-134).

138.   Without changing the position of his right forearm, tori releases his right-hand grip to grasp his own left arm at the bend of the elbow; his left hand is placed at the back of uke's neck. Pressure is applied by pressing with the left hand and pulling back with the right arm.

139.   A front view of the same action.

140

141

CROSS—BODY HAND & ARM LEVER

140.   Tori grips uke's left wrist with his left hand...

141.   raising and turning the captured arm as he...

142.   takes a step with his right foot to place it in front
of uke's feet. As tori steps, he slides his right arm under
uke's captured arm and applies pressure by pushing up
against the elbow with his right upper arm as he pulls

142   143

144

down on uke's captured arm. Uke's hand must be held
palm up.

143.   From the position in photo 142, tori could lever
back against uke's chest with his right arm, putting uke
off balance backward.

144.   Or he could grip cloth at uke's right upper arm and
wheel him around with his left arm and body, putting
uke off balance forward.

BENT—WRIST & ELBOW LOCK

145, 146.   As tori takes a step forward with his right foot, he places his right hand behind uke's right elbow and places the palm of his left hand at the back of uke's right hand.   Raising and bending the captured arm, he applies pressure by pushing down on the elbow and pushing up on the captured hand, using a viselike action; at the same time, tori begins a pivot of 180°...

147, 148.   which is completed as he maintains the two-handed grip on uke's arm.   Tori levers forward to put uke off balance.

145   146

147   148

STRAIGHT—UP ARM LOCK

149.   Tori takes a deep step forward with his left foot and grips uke's right wrist with his left hand...

150.   and reaches over...

151.   around...

152.   and under uke's captured arm to grip his own left wrist as he takes a step with his right foot.

149   **150**

151   **152**

153   154

153.   Tori pivots 180° clockwise as he raises uke's arm with his arms...

154.   and applies pressure by pulling in with his right elbow as he leans forward.

PIVOT & WRIST—TWIST LOCK

155. Tori steps to uke's right and grips uke's right hand with both hands; his thumbs are on the back of uke's hand.

156. Tori swings his right leg outward as he begins...

155

156

157

158

159

160

157. a full 360° pivot, which he executes without releasing his grip. He swings his leg cross-body...

158. to give impetus to his pivot and he raises uke's captured arm as he turns counterclockwise...

159. and twists uke's arm...

160. and ends the pivot and applies pressure by twisting the captured hand.

WHEELING HAND & ARM LEVER

161. Tori grips uke's right wrist with his right hand as he starts a 360° pivot, clockwise...

162. and twists uke's wrist as he raises uke's arm and thrusts his left arm under uke's elbow and pulls down at the captured wrist.

163, 164. Tori maintains both pressures, wheeling uke as he twists the captured arm to put uke off balance.

161

162

163

164

165

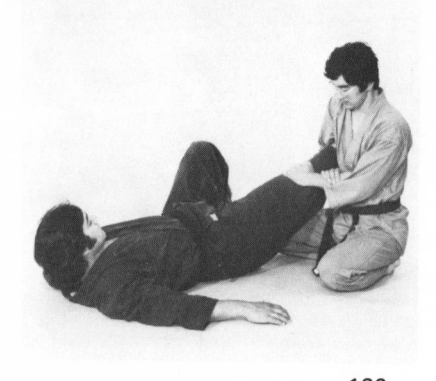

166

ANKLE TWIST, ANKLE LOCK, LEG LOCK

165.   Uke is supine (on his back). Tori grips uke's heel with one hand and the toes of the same foot with the other hand; he twists inward.

166.   Uke is supine. Tori locks uke's ankle under his right arm and places his left hand on uke's shin and grips his own left wrist with his right hand. Tori applies pressure by levering upward with his right forearm and pressing down with his left hand.

Additional pressure is applied if tori leans back somewhat.

167.   Uke is prone (face down on the ground). Tori grips uke's right foot with his left hand and locks it behind uke's left knee and grips uke's left foot with his right hand and applies pressure by levering uke's left leg against his right leg.

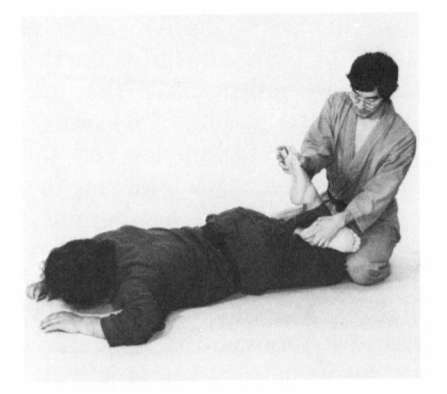

167

HAND & FOOT BLOWS

The diversity of styles among the old jujitsus is nowhere more evident than in the selection and use of hand and foot blows.

Some styles of jujitsu practiced only a few hand and foot blows and relied on them mainly for blocking and feinting. Others emphasized hitting and kicking to such an extent that it would be difficult to distinguish those styles of jujitsu from what we now call karate. The style of karate which we now know as kenpo karate was called Chinese boxing when it was first introduced into Japan and later was called kenpo jujitsu.

The jujitsus which placed heavy emphasis on hand blows were divided into "hard" and "soft" schools. The soft school practiced to develop speed and precision; the hard school practiced to develop maximum power blows. In the hard school, hand and foot conditioning (callusing and desensitizing) was common.

For this book I have made an arbitrary selection of hand and foot blows; included are those which survived in most styles of jujitsu after the introduction of sport judo, karate, and aikido. In karate, the hand and foot blows are primary techniques and there is a greater range and variety of hitting and kicking methods. In sport judo hand and foot blows are not permitted by the rules of contest, even though many judo schools included atemi waza (methods of hitting and kicking) as part of judo instruction. In aikido the hand blows are stylized; they are gestures representing hand blows. Although they were taught in most old style jujitsus, I have not included knee kicks to the groin, eye-gouging, or hand blows to the windpipe. Blows to the eyes or windpipe are very high-risk-of-injury tactics and accidental contact could result in serious injury. Practicing such blows serves no useful purpose for physical fitness and is inappropriate in a recreation activity.

To prevent accidental injury in practice, the safety rules must be strictly observed. No contact is made in the kata application of the hand and foot blows. The objective in practice of the hand and foot blows should be to achieve perfection of technique, without making contact on the practice partner.

HAND BLOWS

168.   The best-known of all the weaponless hand blows used in Asian styles of fighting is the open-hand, slashing blow called the "chop."

169.   Many jujitsu systems used the chop because of its versatility and practicality. It can be used palm up...

170.   or palm down.

It can be used backhanded (as shown) or downward or

168

169

170

upward; it can be used for striking straight out or to the side.

171.   The heel-of-palm blow, commonly used in combination with a backward trip.

172.   Striking up under the jaw with the Y of the hand, also used in combination with a backward trip.

173.   Stabbing finger blows into the side of the neck muscle.   (Stabbing into the eyes or throat of a vicious assailant.)

171

172

173

174.   Fist blows most commonly used in old jujitsu methods were these two: striking with the two large knuckles into bony body surfaces...

175.   or with an extended knuckle into the abdomen or head.

176.   The elbow was used mainly as a blow to the rear, midbody...

177.   or into the head.

174

175

176

177

FOOT BLOWS

Of the many variations of kicks, the most commonly used in old styles of jujitsu were:

178.   Kicking with the ball of the foot.

179.   Kicking with the side of the foot.

178

179

180

181

180. Kicking with the bottom of the foot.
181. Kicking with the heel, to the rear.

182

183

182.   Stamping down with the heel or bottom of the foot.

183.   Kicking with the bottom of the foot, with the hands braced on the floor. Today, this appears to be a highly impractical kick, but when people worked and visited in a kneeling position, the easy shift of weight onto the hands would have made kicking in this manner practical. Now it might be used as a recovery or counter-technique if the defending person has been thrown or has fallen.

TRIPS & THROWS

Most "tricks" in jujitsu end with uke on the ground. The methods used to put him there range from simple to elaborate and difficult. There are trips, pull-downs and lever takedowns; there are complicated lifting, sweeping and over-the-body throws; there are some strange-looking procedures which I strongly doubt were ever applied in real life. Examples of all these categories are included in the following material.

Those who are familiar with sport judo will recognize throwing techniques which are seen in judo competition today, almost identical to their older jujitsu forms. The trips and sweeps commonly used in jujitsu systems are now taught in many styles of karate. The hand and lever throws can be recognized as the forerunners of aikido as it is currently practiced.

Early styles of jujitsu were practiced in rough and tumble fashion. Injury was common. Students threw each other without regard for safety. Skilled students threw novice students violently. Novices were not taught breakfalls and if they survived the dangers of first-year practice, inflicted the same kind of harsh treatment on new students when they became more skilled.

In some jujitsu systems, and in some jujitsu books published in English at the beginning of the twentieth century, the hazards of practicing throwing techniques with a partner were acknowledged; in others they were ignored. Some schools introduced safety falls and some put considerable emphasis on learning the falls before practicing throws and takedowns.

A significant distinction between sport judo and jujitsu is that participants in a judo match are protected from injury by the rules of the game and the method of training and practice which includes rigorous falling training. Deliberate use of a throwing technique or a throwing tactic likely to hurt or injure an opponent player is a foul in a judo match and is subject to penalty. Hitting and kicking are prohibited in judo, whereas in jujitsu it is assumed that a hand or foot blow will be used to hurt, or at least distract, the adversary before a throw or takedown is applied. In jujitsu the objective is to incapacitate an adversary.

The presentation of jujitsu in this book is modified for safe practice. Since there are no sporting rules for jujitsu, the method of training and mutual concern for safety are the important safeguards for today's students. Rough throwing is inappropriate in physical fitness/recreation activity. Only those who have been taught safety falls should perform the throws and trips as they are illustrated in this book. A guide to safety falls can be found in my judo book.*

An alternate procedure for practicing the jujitsu trips and falls is for partners to ease or set each other down carefully, tori giving support to uke until uke is safely on the ground. Because jujitsu is often practiced on bare floors, without protective mats, care in putting uke down is particularly important. It is possible to practice all the movements and techniques in the jujitsu katas without vigorous throwing and that is the only safe way for novices to practice; it is the only safe way for people to practice who do not know the breakfalls. A high level of technical skills in performing the katas is not likely to be reached until both partners can take falls without danger of injury.

---

*Tegner, Bruce. 1975. Bruce Tegner's Complete Book of Judo. Ventura: Thor Publishing Company.

UNDER–JAW THRUST with LEG BLOCK

184.   As tori takes a deep step in with his right foot to place it behind uke's right leg, he grips uke's right wrist with his left hand and thrusts up under uke's jaw with the Y of his right hand.

185.   Pulling with his left hand and following through with the right-hand thrust, tori puts uke into off-balance position, back.

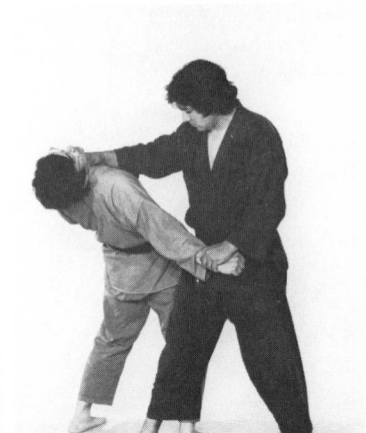

184   185

ARM LEVER & BACKWARD TRIP

186.   Tori steps around to uke's side and thrusts his right arm across uke's chest as he places his right leg between uke's legs, buckling uke's left knee with his right leg.

187.   He trips uke around and back by follow-through arm action which trips uke over his leg.

186   187

KICKBACK THROW

188.   Tori grips uke in the standard starting position.

189.   As he takes a deep step in with his left foot to place it next to uke's right foot, tori tilts uke with a wheeling action, around and back, to put uke into poor balance.

190.   Tori continues wheeling uke around and down as he kicks uke's right leg out from under him with a swinging, calf-to-calf, straight-leg kick with carry-through...

191.   to put uke on the ground. Tori is in position to apply a restraining hold.

188

189

190

191

ARM—TWIST TAKEDOWN

192.   Tori crosses his arms and grips uke's wrists and...

193.   crosses uke's arms and twists uke's arms sharply...

194, 195.   to take uke to the ground.

192

193

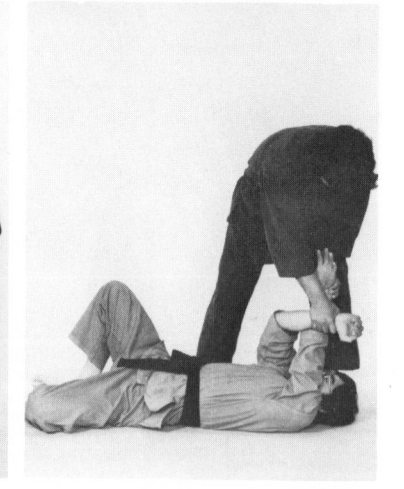

194

195

STRAIGHT—LEG THROW

196.   From the standard starting position...

197.   tori pivots on his left foot and places his extended, straight right leg in back of uke's right foot, ankle to ankle, and wheels uke around with his arms...

198.   and down onto the ground. Tori is in position to apply a hold.

196

197

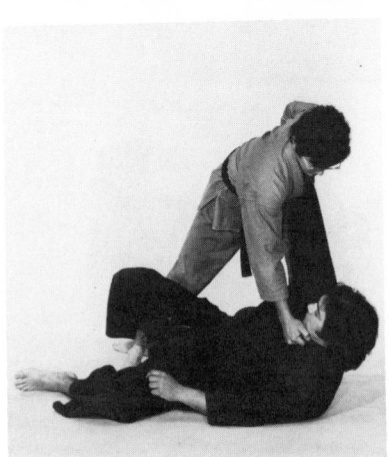

198

PULLING—DOWN STRAIGHT—LEG THROW

199.　From the standard starting position, tori pivots on his right foot, stepping counterclockwise with his left foot...

200.　and drops onto his left knee as he tilts uke around and down...

201.　and places his straight right leg at uke's right leg, ankle to ankle, as he continues the wheeling action...

202.　to put uke on the ground. Tori is in position to apply a hold.

199

200

201

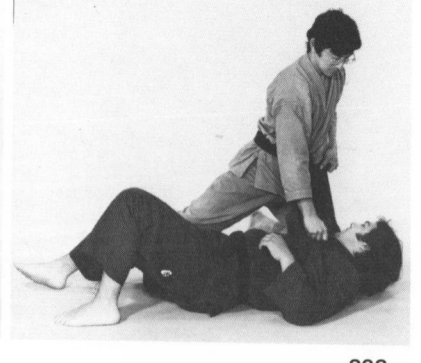

202

BACK SWEEPING—FOOT THROW

203. From the standard starting position, tori uses arm action to twist uke back and around...

204. off balance, as he positions his left foot behind uke's right foot...

205. and as he sweeps uke's right leg up, he pulls sharply around and down with his arms...

206. to put uke on the ground. Tori is in position to apply a hold.

203

204

205

206

HIP THROW

207.   From the standard starting position...

208.   tori steps across with his right foot to place it in front of uke's right foot and pivots counterclockwise to position his right hip at uke's right thigh.

209.   With a combination of wheeling arm movement and a springing-up hip movement, he pulls uke onto his right hip...

210.   and around, down and over. Tori is in position to apply a hold.

207

208

209

210

PULLING—DOWN THROW

211.   This technique was used in many systems of jujitsu and was taught as a response to a back body grab. Tori takes a deep breath to expand the grip somewhat...

212.   and grips cloth at uke's right shoulder as he starts to do gown...

213.   onto his left knee and grips uke's right wrist.

214.   He wheels uke around and over his bent leg, taking him to the ground.

211

212

213

214

PULLING—DOWN HAND THROW

215.   From the standard starting position, tori begins to pivot counterclockwise as he grips uke's right wrist...

216.   with both hands and uses the momentum of his body to pull uke forward...

217.   and off balance; tori drops to his left knee and continues to pull uke over...

218.   onto the ground. Tori kneels at uke's side, in position to apply a hold.

215

216

217

218

BODY—SQUEEZE THROW

219.　　From the standard starting position...

220.　　tori pivots counterclockwise...

221.　　and slides his arm around uke's neck and topples him over his back, face down. Tori grips cloth at his own upper right leg with his right hand.

222.　　With his left hand, tori reaches over uke's leg and grips cloth. He applies pressure by pulling his arms together. Tori completes the throw by wheeling around and down with his upper body to put uke on the ground, on his side.

219

220

221

222

REVERSE HIP THROW

223.   From the standard starting position, tori takes a step to uke's right side with his left foot...

224.   and then steps around counterclockwise with his right foot to place his hips at uke's hips...

225.   and slides his right arm around uke's neck and topples uke across his back, face up. He reaches over uke's right leg and grips cloth with his left hand.

226.   Tori applies pressure by pulling inward with both arms. He completes the throw by wheeling around and down to put uke on the ground, on his side.

223

224

225

226

UPSIDE–DOWN THROW

227.   Tori (shown left) grips cloth high at uke's left shoulder with his right hand; his thumb is inside the garment.

228.   With his right hand, tori reaches between uke's legs and grips his belt at the back...

229.   and wheels him over by pushing with his left hand as he pulls and lifts with his right hand.

227   228

In a kata routine, uke would be put on the ground on his back.

229

LEG TAKEDOWN

230. Tori grips uke's ankle with both hands and places his shoulder against uke's knee...

231. to put uke on the ground by pulling sharply upward on the captured ankle as he pushes with his shoulder.

230

231

ANKLE THROW

This technique, found in many systems of jujitsu, was usually shown as a response to an under-arms grab.

232.　Tori sidesteps with his right foot and leans forward...

233.　to grip uke's ankle with both hands...

234.　and pull sharply up and around to wheel uke...

235.　down onto the ground. Tori maintains his hold on uke's ankle.

232

233

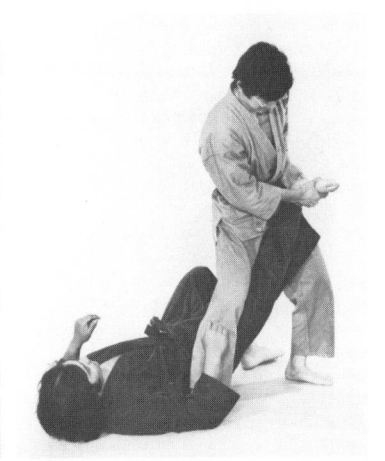

234

235

LEG LEVER TAKEDOWN

236.   Tori is on the ground. He places his right foot at uke's knee and hooks his left foot behind uke's ankle...

237.   to take uke off balance by pushing with his right foot as he pulls and lifts with his left foot.

He follows through to take uke to the ground.

236

237

KATAS

A kata is a prearranged, rehearsed series of movements. The kata is also called a "form" or a "dance" or a "formal routine."

Katas evolved from ways of practicing the martial arts. One form of practice was purely an exercise in which the individuals went through the motions of hitting and kicking actions in a manner resembling shadow boxing or practiced single techniques together (wazas) to develop proficiency. Another form of practice was like sparring; the opponents practiced together with as much realism as suited their style.

Two distinct activities grew out of these two forms of practice -- contest (shiai) and kata, with an intermediate free-style practice (randori) found in judo.

Kata forms are practiced in many of the martial arts systems. There are solo forms and there are two-man forms. In jujitsu the principal katas are for two people.

In the jujitsu katas, all of the elements are brought together. From the simulated attack, through the escape or counterblow, through the trip or throw, to the ending hold or lock, the movements are flowing, graceful, stylish and handsome. Whereas the earlier practice is a repetition of a single technique to learn the correct procedure, kata practice is repetition of the combinations of movements so that transition from one action to the next is made easily, without hesitation and with technical perfection as the goal.

Individuals who have had previous experience in the martial arts will note the absence of techniques which were popular in old-style jujitsu katas, among them the knee kick into the groin. The omission of the groin kick is deliberate. Young people and women are increasingly showing an interest in practicing the martial arts for physical fitness and for self-defense. It is my belief that kicking into the groin is not a technique which should be encouraged among young people since it is unnecessarily violent for most of the situations in which it is shown as a defense. Although girls and women are indoctrinated to think that a kick into the groin is practical self-defense, most of them prefer not to use the technique because they find it repugnant. In my experience, most women and girls are relieved to know that there are alternative defenses which are effective and more useful to them in many of the assault situations they are likely to encounter.

As I have mentioned before, ancient forms of two-man practice were rough and often dangerous. In contrast, present-day forms of kata emphasize perfection of technique and safety in practice. Partners do not make contact when they simulate the hand and foot blows. The holds and locks are applied with correct form but without force. Since both partners rehearse the kata, uke is not taken by surprise and can respond by going with tori's action, instead of resisting it, and thus avoid injury. Partners who do not know safe falling techniques must not throw or trip each other, but may carefully ease each other down, using those trips and throws which lend themselves to this mode of practice.

When all of the pictured katas have been learned and can be performed smoothly and elegantly, a high level of technical skill will have been achieved. Those who wish to go beyond what is shown can practice variations of the katas illustrated. For instance, where hand blows are simulated, foot blows can be substituted. Choose from among the kicks in photos 178 to 182 and use those which are appropriate and possible in the given situation. Another way of enhancing and developing skill is to improvise different combinations of techniques and make up your own katas.

Partners take turns playing the role of tori and uke.

Practice of jujitsu is started and ended with a simple bow. This is a gesture of courtesy at greeting and parting. It is the Japanese equivalent of shaking hands. For kata practice, the bowing is more formal.

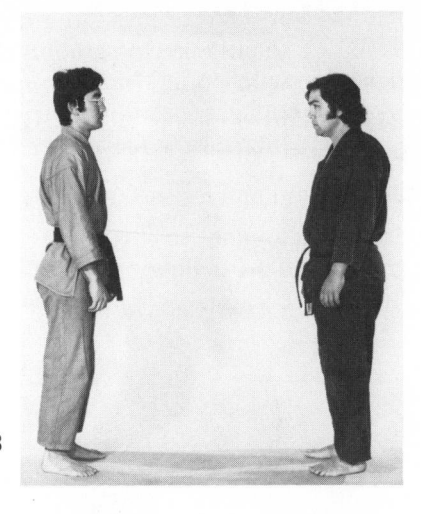

238

239

238, 239. Partners face each other at a distance of about two meters. They place their hands at their thighs and bow from the waist.

At the end of the kata practice session, they bow in the same manner before leaving the mat.

ARM BAR KATA

240.   Uke attacks by grabbing tori (cloth) high at the right side with his left hand.

241.   Tori responds with a slash into the face as he grips uke's wrist with his left hand...

242.   and applies the arm bar (photos 38-40)...

243.   dropping to his right knee to put uke on the ground. Tori maintains the pressure, pulling inward with his right forearm.

240

241

242

243

STRAIGHT—DOWN ARM LOCK KATA

244. Uke strikes out with an open-hand blow with his right hand; tori parries downward at the wrist...

245. and steps in with his right foot behind uke's right foot as he applies a straight-down arm lock (photos 47-49)...

246. and twists and trips uke back...

247. and down onto the ground; as uke falls, tori drops onto his right knee and maintains the lock.

244

245

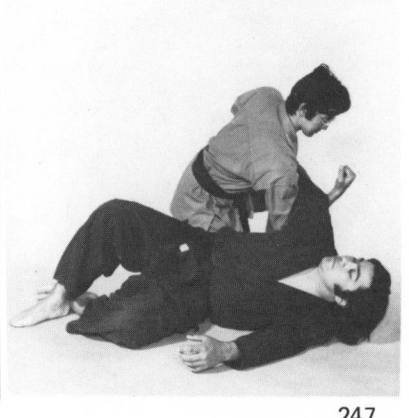

246   247

ESCAPE/INWARD WRIST LOCK KATAS

248.   Uke grips tori's right wrist with his left hand.

249.   Tori twists his arm up and out...

250.   to free it; he grips uke's hand and...

251.   applies an inward wrist lock (photos 24-26). Tori
takes uke to the ground.

248

249

250

251

252, 253.   Another kata with the same ending begins
with a wrist grip from behind.   Tori wheels counterclockwise, and twisting his right wrist...

254, 255.   he completes the pivot and frees his wrists.
Gripping uke's hand with his left hand, he then applies an
inward wrist lock (photos 24-26).   Tori takes uke to the
ground.

252

253

254

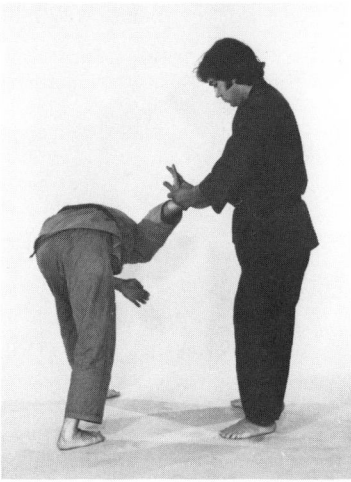

255

256   257

WRIST—GRIP ESCAPE & HAND LOCK KATA

256.   Uke grips tori's wrists.

257.   Tori twists and releases his left hand...

258.   and grips uke's left wrist with his left hand and twists his...

259.   right hand free of uke's grasp.

260.   Tori grips uke's left hand at the fingers...

261.   and applies a hand lock (photos 27, 28).

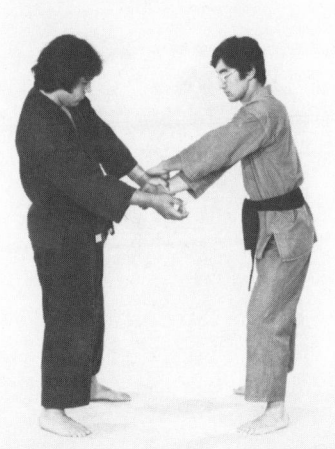

258

259

260

261

262   263

BENT—ARM HOLD & BAR KATA

262.   Uke grabs tori with his right hand.

263.   Tori grips the wrist and elbow...

264.   and pivots into position to apply the bent-arm hold...

265.   and bar (photos 79-81).

266.   Tori follows through with the bar pressure and drops onto his left knee to take uke to the ground; tori applies pressure by clamping in with his left hand and pushing uke's bent wrist toward his head.

264

265

266

OUTWARD WRIST LOCK KATA

267.   Uke attempts a clawing hand-blow attack, which tori parries at the wrist.

268.   He applies an outward wrist lock (photos 20-23)...

269.   and uses a kickback throw (photos 188-191) to put uke on the ground.

270.   Tori steps across uke's captured arm with his right foot and braces it next to uke's neck as he maintains pressure on the captured hand.

267

268

269

270

INWARD WRIST LOCK KATA

271.   Uke attempts a high grab. Tori captures the reaching hand with both his hands...

272.   and twists the captured hand, as he pivots...

273.   and applies an inward wrist lock (photos 24-26).

271

272   273

274

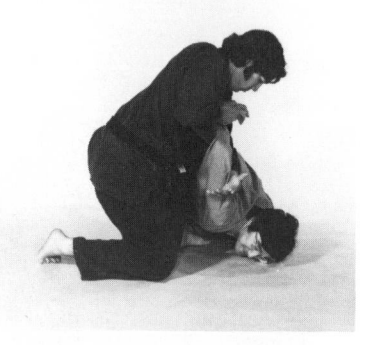

275

274.   By applying downward pressure with his hands and body, tori puts uke on the ground...

275.   and drops onto his right knee. He maintains pressure on uke's hand with his right hand and braces his left hand at uke's upper arm.

LEG LOCK KATA

276.   Uke kicks at tori.

277.   Tori captures the kicking foot...

276

277

278

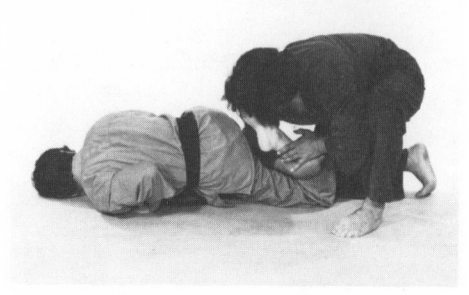

279

278.   and twists it to turn uke around, face down...

279.   and drops to his right knee to take uke to the
ground and applies a leg lock (photo 167).

LEG TAKEDOWN KATA

280.   As uke steps forward to attack, tori grips his ankle...

281.   and applies the leg takedown (photos 230, 231)...

280

281

282. maintaining his hold on the ankle to apply an ankle twist...

283. or an ankle lock (photo 166).

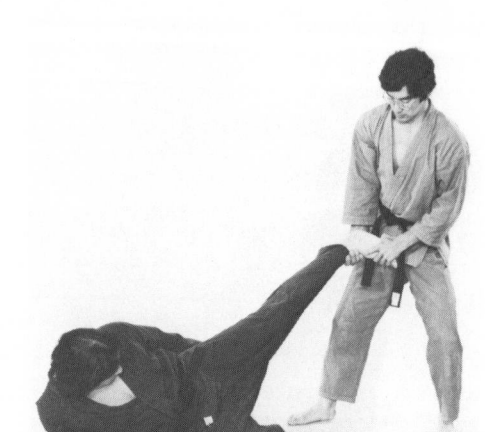

282

283

HAND & ARM LEVER KATA

284.   Uke grips tori's left wrist with his left hand.

285.   Tori strikes with a right-handed slash...

286.   and twists his wrist free and grips and raises uke's left arm and thrusts his right arm under it to apply the cross-body hand and arm lever (photos 140-144)...

284

285   286

287. carrying through with his right-arm thrust and tripping uke with a back sweeping-foot throw (photos 203-206)...

288. to put him on the ground; tori drops to his right knee and turns his hand palm down to brace it at uke's belt; he levers uke's arm (palm up) across his arm.

287

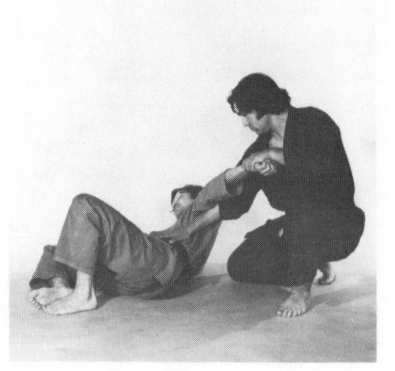

288

HAND & ARM HOLD with HEAD PRESSURE KATA

289. Uke (shown right) attempts an open-hand attack. Tori grips the wrist...

290. and pulls and twists uke's arm as he strikes into uke's midbody...

291. and applies the hand and arm hold with head pressure (photos 66-67).

289

290   291

292.   By thrusting down at uke's head and pulling and twisting uke's captured arm...

293.   tori puts uke on the ground.

292

293

UNDER ARM PIN KATA

294.   Uke attacks with an open-hand blow, using his right hand, palm up; tori blocks with his right forearm...

295.   and applies an under arm pin (photos 73-75)...

296.   and positions his right foot behind uke's right foot to trip uke back...

297.   and onto the ground.

294

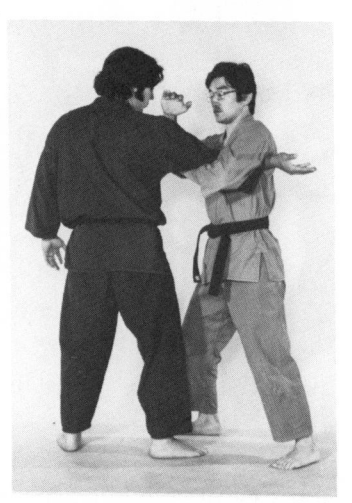

295

296

297

298   299

HAND LOCK/OVER—SHOULDER LOCK KATA

298. Uke attempts a high reaching attack. Tori grips the reaching hand and wrist and...

299. applies a hand lock with arm brace (photos 29-31); then he...

300. pivots as he draws uke's arm over his shoulder to apply an over-shoulder lock (photos 32-35), and...

301. wheels uke around; tori extends his left leg and...

302. trips uke down and around his left leg...

303. putting uke on the ground. Tori goes down onto his left knee and draws uke's right arm across his thigh and applies an arm bar (photos 38-40) over uke's captured arm.

300

301

302

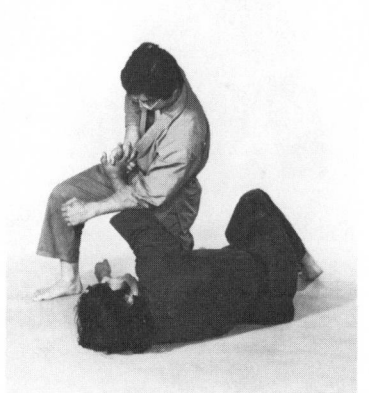

303

WHEELING HAND & ARM LEVER KATA

304.   Uke attempts a reaching attack with his right hand; tori grips the reaching wrist with his right hand, palm up...

305.   he pivots and...

306.   applies a wheeling hand and arm lever (photos 161-164)...

307.   and as uke loses his balance forward, tori drops onto his left knee and repositions his left arm at the back of uke's captured upper arm. He applies pressure by pushing down with his left arm and pulling up on the captured hand.

304

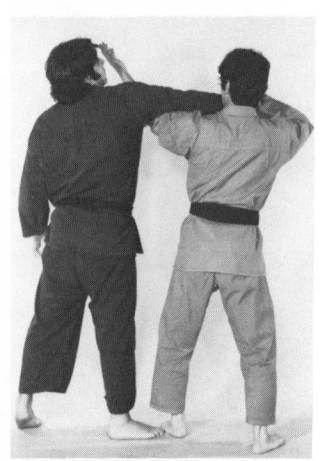

305

306

307

ARM LEVER & BACKWARD TRIP KATA

308.   Uke attacks with an over-arms body grab from behind.   Tori takes a deep breath as he flings his arms outward to loosen uke's grip...

309.   and pivots clockwise to place his right leg behind uke's left leg...

310.   and applies an arm lever and backward trip (photos 186, 187) to take...

311.   uke to the ground.

308

309

310

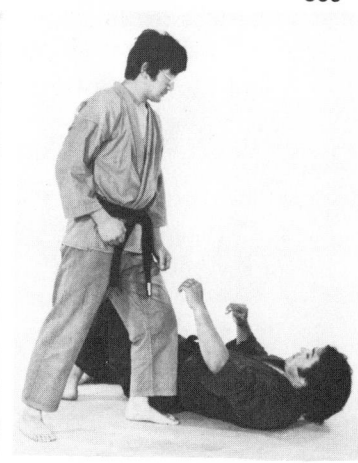

311

312   313

STRAIGHT—ARM LOCK KATA

312.   Uke grips cloth high at tori's right side with his left hand.

313.   Tori strikes an open-hand slash with his right hand and grips the wrist with his left hand...

314.   and pivots into position to apply a straight-arm lock (photos 68-72).

315.   By pulling the captured arm across his body as he places his right leg in front of uke's legs, tori puts uke into forward off-balance position...

316.   and takes him to the ground, where he applies an arm bar (photos 38-40).

314

315

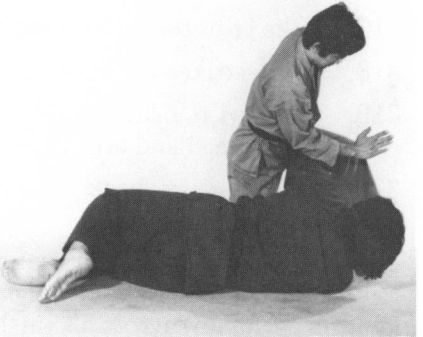

316

317   318

HEAD & ARM TWIST KATA

317.   Uke grips tori's left wrist with his left hand.

318.   Tori strikes an open-hand blow into uke's face...

319.   and twists his captured wrist free, grips uke's wrist and applies a head and arm twist (photos 54-57)...

320.   and uses a back sweeping-foot throw (photos 203-206)...

321.   to put uke on the ground. Tori drops onto his right knee; he maintains the head twist, and levers uke's left arm (palm up) across his thigh.

319

320

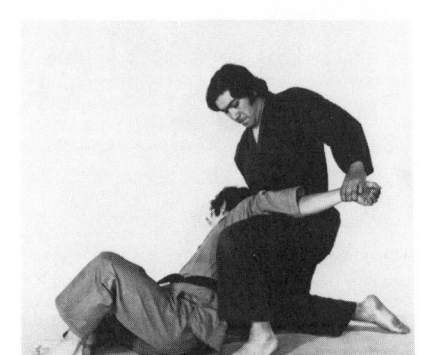

321

HAND LOCK with ARM BRACE KATA

322. Uke attempts a high-reaching attack. Tori grips the reaching hand and strikes at the elbow with his left hand...

323. and applies a hand lock with arm brace (photos 29-31)...

322

323

324.   uses a back sweeping-foot throw (photos 203-206)...

325.   to put uke on the ground. Tori braces his left knee at uke's elbow and maintains pressure on the captured hand.

324

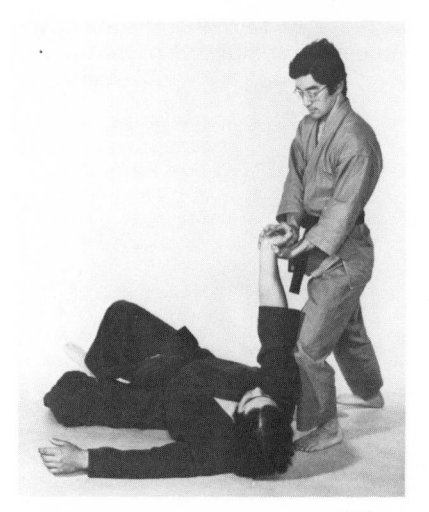

325

326   327

HAND LOCK KATA

326.   Uke attacks with a palm-up slash...

327.   which tori blocks and grabs.

328.   Tori applies a hand lock (photos 27-78)...

329.   and uses a kickback throw (photos 188-191)...

330.   to put uke on the ground; tori drops to his right
knee and maintains pressure on the hand.

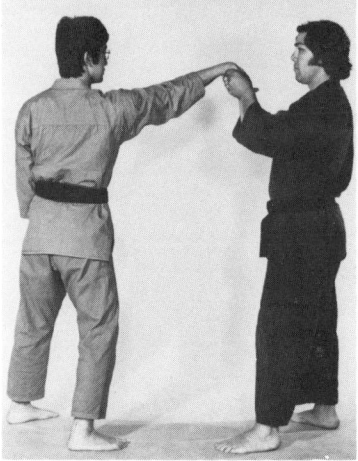

328

329

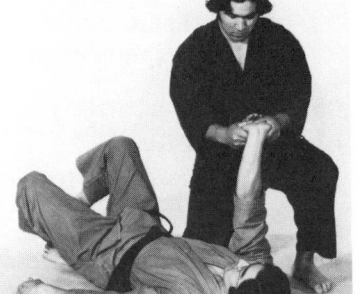

330

331   332

ELBOW, WRIST & SHOULDER LOCK KATA

331.   Uke grips tori's left wrist.

332.   Tori twists out of uke's grasp and...

333.   grips the back of uke's hand and

334.   uke's shoulder and applies...

335.   the elbow, wrist and shoulder lock (photos 76-78), driving uke down...

336.   onto the ground; tori drops onto his right knee and maintains pressure on the arm.

333

334

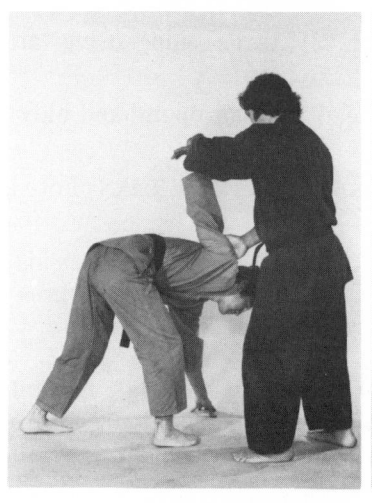

335

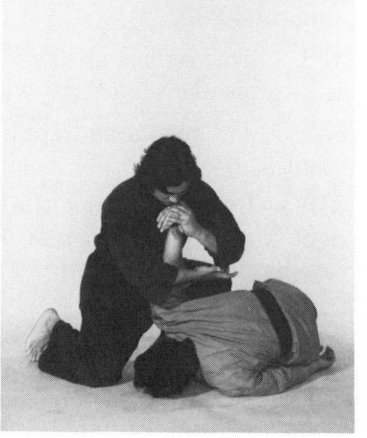

336

337   338

UPPER ARM LOCK KATA

337.   Uke grabs cloth high at tori's side, using an unnatural grip.

338.   Tori strikes at uke's head with an open-hand blow as he grips uke's left wrist with his left hand...

339.   and pivots and applies an upper arm lock (photos 58-60).

340.   By maintaining the lock and dropping onto his right knee, tori takes uke to the ground; he applies pressure by pulling the captured arm toward uke's head.

341.   Uke grabs cloth at tori's right side, using a natural grip. Tori grips uke's wrist with his right hand and places the fingers of his left hand on uke's hand and his thumb at the first joint of uke's thumb.

342.   By squeezing with his left hand, tori effects release.

He applies an upper arm lock and takes uke to the ground (photos 339, 340).

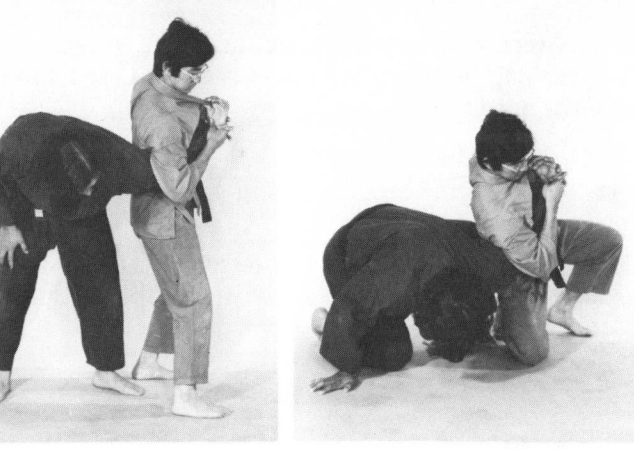

339

340

341

342

STRAIGHT—UP ARM LOCK KATA

343.   Uke attempts to grab tori's left wrist; tori grips the reaching wrist as he strikes a backhanded blow with his right hand...

344.   and steps into position to grip uke's arm...

345.   and pivots around to apply a straight-up arm lock (photos 149-154).

346.   Applying downward pressure with his arms and dropping onto his left knee, tori takes uke to the ground.

343

344

345

346

347   348

CHOKE HOLD with ARM PRESSURE KATA

347.   Uke chokes tori.

348.   Tori breaks the choke with an upward arm-thrust...

349.   and starts to spin uke...

350.   around into position for the application of...

351.   a choke hold with arm pressure (photos 138, 139)...

352.   and takes uke to the ground by pulling back and down with his arms as he goes down onto his right knee.

349

350

351

352

353   354

WRIST & ELBOW LOCK KATA

353.   Uke strikes with an upward knuckle punch...

354.   and tori slashes with his left hand and grabs the hand with his right hand and...

355.   raises the captured hand; he begins to apply pressure and...

356.   pivots around to uke's side and applies a wrist and elbow lock (photos 99-103)...

357.   levering forward and down...

358.   to put uke on the ground; tori twists uke's captured arm up his back.

355

356

357

358

 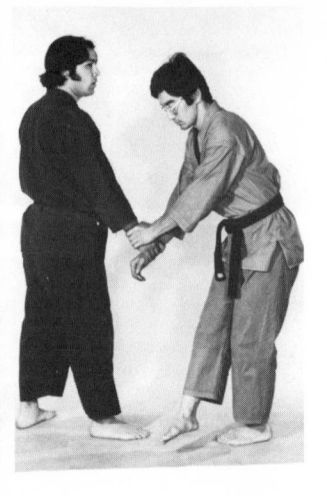

359   360

PIVOT & WRIST—TWIST LOCK KATA

359.   Uke grips tori's right wrist with his right hand.

360.   Tori grips the wrist with his left hand as he begins the pivot...

361.   frees his captured wrist...

362.   and completes the pivot and applies an arm-twist lock (photos 107-113 or 155-160) with follow-through to bend uke forward...

363.   and repositions his left arm at the back of uke's elbow.

364.   Tori puts uke on the ground by applying arm-bar pressure and by bending his knees sharply. He maintains the bar pressure and continues to pull up at uke's wrist (uke's hand is palm up).

361

362

363

364

365   366

ESCAPE/OUTWARD WRIST LOCK KATA

365.   Uke attacks by pulling tori's arm up his back.

366.   Tori begins to pivot clockwise...

367.   as he raises his arm

368.   and continues the pivot...

369.   to face uke and grip uke's left hand with his left hand...

370.   and twist his captured hand free and apply an outward wrist lock (photos 20-23).

Tori takes uke to the ground.

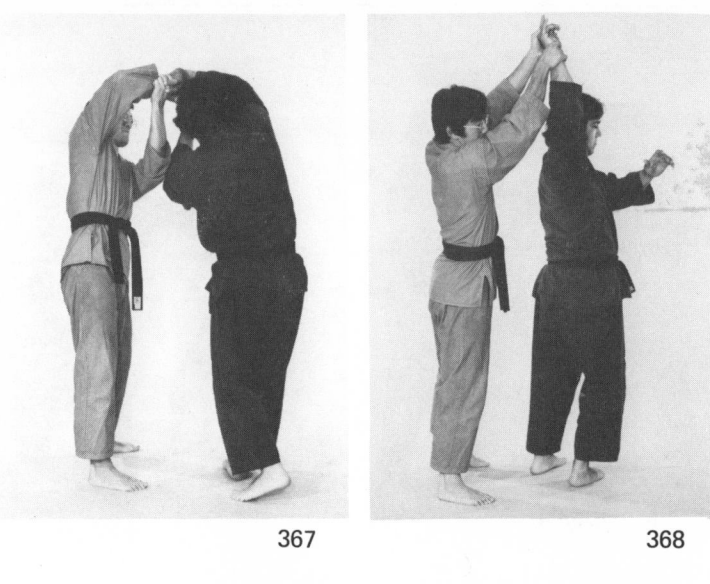

367

369

368

370

371   372

BENT—ARM LEVER with PIVOT KATA

371.   Uke starts a high grab.

372.   Tori grips the reaching wrist with both hands and pulls uke forward...

373.   as he pivots...

374.   to apply a bent-arm lever lock (photos 114-119) and then...

375.   places his right leg behind uke's right leg, repositions his right hand to apply an elbow lever (photos 96-98), and trips uke back...

376.   and onto the ground. As uke falls, tori drops onto his right knee. He maintains the elbow lever.

373

374

375

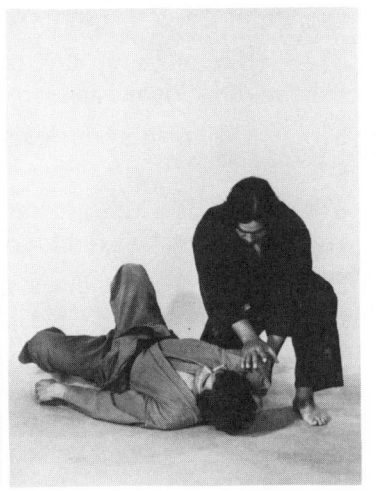

376

377   378

ESCAPE/BENT—ARM LEVER with PIVOT KATA

377.   Uke moves around behind tori and grips tori's right wrist with his right hand.

378.   Tori pivots clockwise as he pulls uke's gripping arm...

379.   and uses the momentum of his body to assist his pivot; he grips uke's right wrist with his left hand...

380.   as he raises uke's arm and twists and frees his captured wrist...

381.   and completes the pivot and applies a bent-arm lever (photos 114-119) and then...

382.   shifts his right hand into position to apply an elbow lever (photos 96-98).

He follows through, levering the captured arm back and down and takes uke to the ground.

379

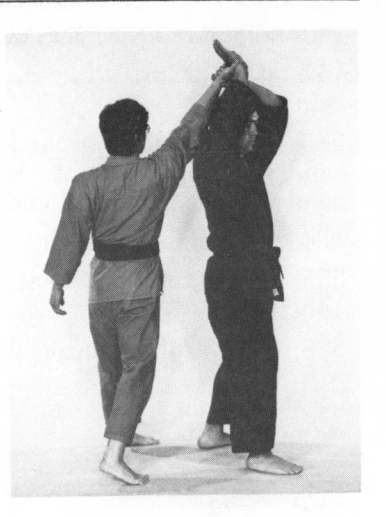

380

381

382

ESCAPE/BENT—WRIST & ELBOW LOCK KATA

Uke attacks tori with an under-arms body grab from behind.

383.   Tori reaches around uke's right arm with his right hand and grips cloth at uke's elbow; he grips uke's right hand with his left hand and applies a squeezing pressure...

384.   which he maintains as he pivots clockwise...

385.   and applies a bent-wrist and elbow lock (photos 145-148)...

386.   with follow-through to take uke to the ground.

383

384

385

386

ESCAPE/STRAIGHT–UP ARM LOCK KATA

Uke attacks with an under-arms body grab.

387.   Tori grips uke's left wrist with his right hand and with his left hand he reaches under uke's left arm and grips his own right wrist.

388.   As he twists his body sharply around counter-clockwise, he thrusts with his arms to break the grip...

389.   and he completes the pivot...

390.   to apply a straight-up arm lock (photos 149-154). He takes uke to the ground.

387   388

389   390

391

BENT—ARM LEVER LOCK KATA

391.   Uke attempts a wrist-grip attack. Tori grabs the reaching wrist with his left hand and slashes onto the arm.

392.   He applies a bent-arm lever lock (photos 61-65)...

393.   and, maintaining pressure at the captured arm, he effects a kickback throw (photos 188-191)...

394.   to put uke on the ground.

395.   Tori drops onto his right knee, repositions his right hand and applies an elbow lever (photos 96-98).

392

393

394

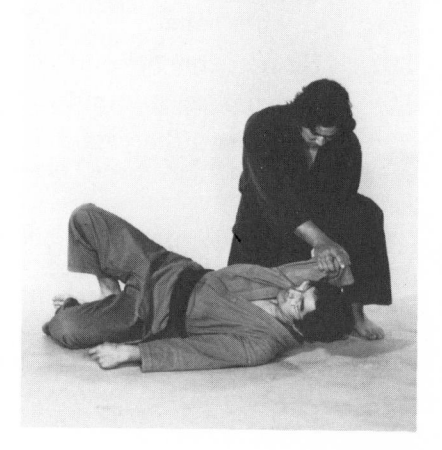

395

396   397

PIVOT & ARM TWIST KATA

396.   Uke starts a high-reaching attack. Tori grips the wrist with both hands.

397.   He starts the pivot...

398.   and applies an arm-twist lock (photos 107-113)...

399.   and draws the captured arm up uke's back as he reaches around uke's neck, places his hand on uke's right shoulder...

400.   and pulls him back and down onto the ground; tori drops onto his right knee, maintains the arm lock and applies choking pressure with his left forearm.

398

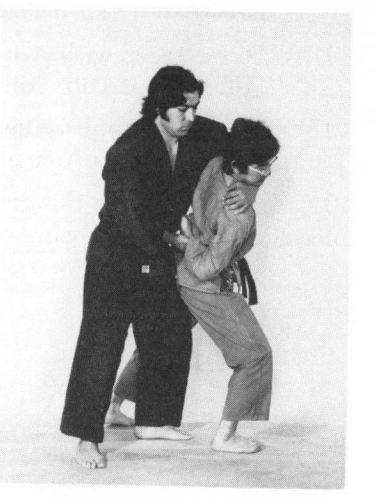

399

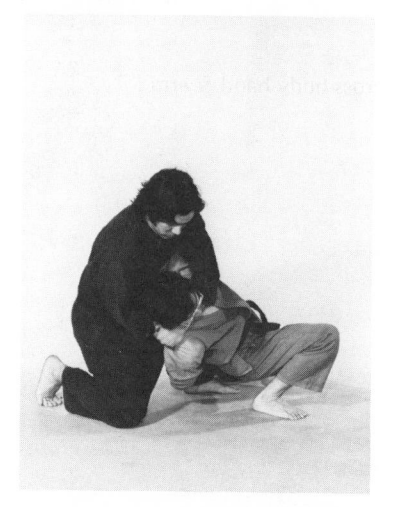

400

STRAIGHT—ARM RESTRAINING HOLD KATA

401.   Uke attacks with a high slash. Tori parries the arm with a slash (photos 168, 169)...

402, 403.   and applies the straight-arm restraining hold (photos 82-85) with sufficient pressure...

404.   to put uke on the ground; tori drops onto his left knee and maintains pressure on the arm.

401

402

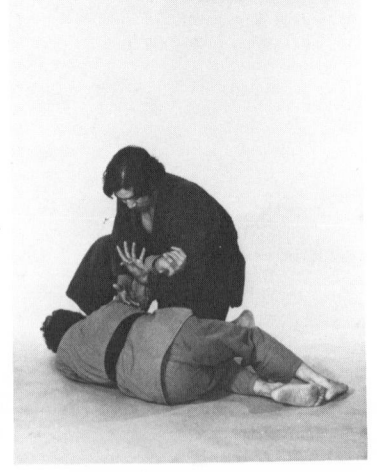

403   404

CHOKE HOLD with KNUCKLE PRESSURE KATA

405.   Uke punches.

406.   Tori parries the punch and counters with a knuckle blow (photo 175).

407.   He grips uke and...

408.   applies a choke hold with knuckle pressure (photos 138, 139), pulling him back and...

405

406

407

408

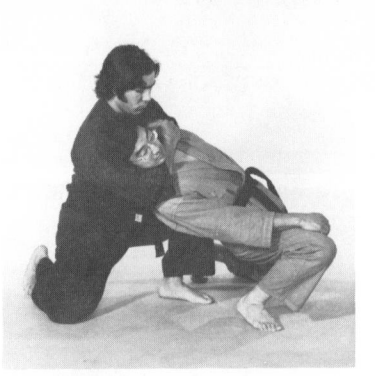

409. down onto the ground as he drops to his right knee with his left knee into uke's back.

FRONT BENT—ARM LOCK KATA

410. Uke attempts a hammer blow. Tori blocks it and...

411

412

413

414

411.   grips the wrist...

412.   and applies a front bent-arm lock (photos 92-95) in a variation in which the hand positions are reversed.

413.   He applies a kickback throw (photos 188-191)...

414.   and drops onto his right knee as he puts uke on the ground and applies an elbow lever (photos 96-98).

BENT—ARM RESTRAINING HOLD KATA

415.   Uke attacks with a low punch; tori parries and grabs the reaching arm...

416.   pivots...

417.   and applies a bent-arm restraining hold (photos 86-89).

418.   Tori puts uke on the ground by applying arm pressure over and down as he drops onto his right knee.

415

416

417

418

ESCAPE/STRAIGHT—ARM RESTRAINING HOLD KATA

Uke attacks with an over-arms body grab from behind.

419.   Tori takes a deep breath as he flings his arms upward to loosen uke's grip...

420.   and he ducks down and pivots clockwise...

421.   to escape and begins to apply...

422.   a straight-arm restraining hold (photos 82-85). He takes uke to the ground.

419

420

421

422

ESCAPE/BENT—ARM RESTRAINING HOLD/WRIST LOCK KATA

Uke attacks with an over-arms body grab from behind. Tori escapes as in photos 418 and 419...

423.   and applies a bent-arm restraining hold with wrist lock (photos 90, 91).

424.   He takes uke to the ground.

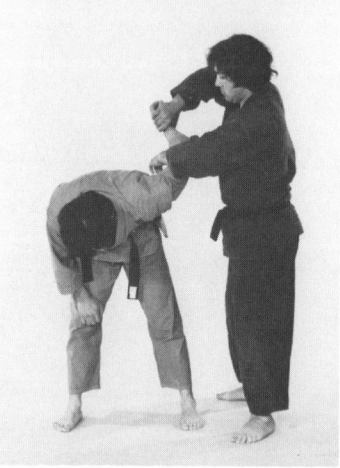
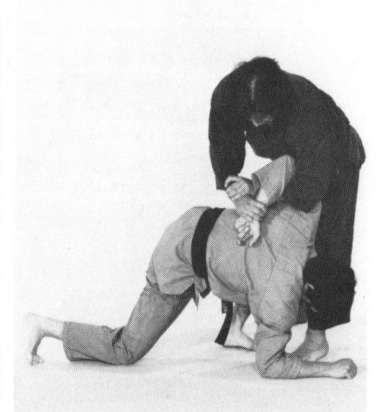

423   424

BETWEEN—LEG ARM LOCK KATA

425.   Uke punches low. Tori grips the wrist and...

426.   pulls uke forward...

427.   and applies the lock (photos 120-124) with carry-through, pushing at uke's back...

425

426   427

428

428. to put him on the ground.

429. Tori drops down onto his left knee, drawing uke's arm across his right thigh; he levers down on the captured arm.

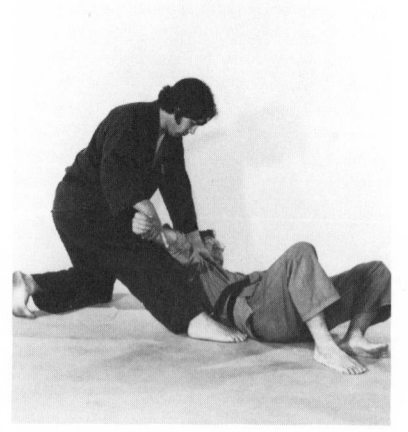

429

BODY—SQUEEZE THROW KATA

430. Uke attempts a choke attack; tori avoids the choke with upthrust arms...

431. and begins to pivot and slide his arm around uke's neck...

432. into position to apply...

433. a body-squeeze throw (photos 219-222)...

430

431

432

433

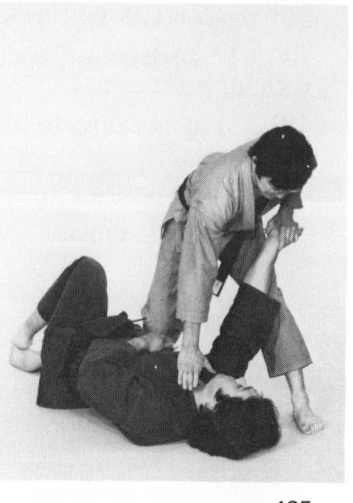

434   435

434.   with follow-through...

435.   to put uke on the ground. As uke falls, tori drops
onto his right knee; he braces his right hand at uke's chest
and draws uke's right arm across his thigh.

REVERSE HIP THROW KATA

436. Uke attempts a hammer-blow attack, which tori parries at the wrist.

437. Tori grips the wrist and pulls as he pivots counter-clockwise to place himself...

436

437

438

439

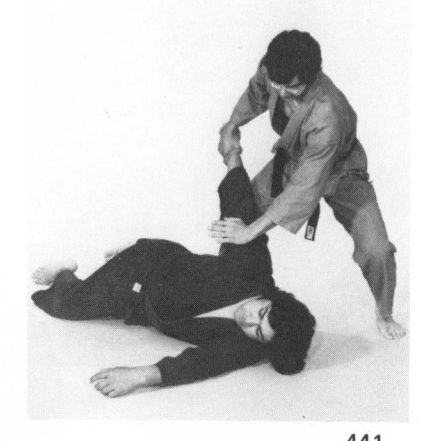

440

441

438.   back-to-back with uke as he slides his arm around uke's neck...

439.   and squats into position...

440.   to apply a reverse hip throw (photos 223-226)...

441.   with follow-through to put uke on the ground, on his side. Tori draws uke's right arm (palm up) across his bent right leg as he strikes an open-hand blow into the side of uke's neck.

KNEELING & SWORD KATAS

The carrying and use of swords, daggers and other knife weapons was common in feudal Japan and defenses against them were found in many styles of jujitsu. Attack-and-defense practice developed into highly stylized routines with elaborate etiquette and rigid, formal procedures.

Kneeling katas were found in all styles of jujitsu practiced in Japan at the end of the last century, reflecting the cultural patterns of the age when many social, business and recreational activities were carried on from a kneeling posture.

In the jujitsu books intended for Western readers, the kneeling katas and kneeling attack-and-defense tricks were rarely shown. But Kano adopted kneeling katas for the self-defense aspect of judo as part of the instruction given to advanced students. Kneeling kata practice in judo schools persisted far beyond the era in which it might have had some practical value.

There were many other kinds of weapons used in various styles of jujitsu, including farm implements adapted to hand-to-hand combat, sticks of many kinds, including the short yawara hand stick and the medium yawara stick, which resembles a police baton. There were katas showing sticks for defense, katas in which the assailant uses a stick and the defense is weaponless, and there were katas in which both attacker and defender were stick-armed. A few of the jujitsu books showed stick defenses against fire-arms, with apparently no recognition of the capabilities of the gun -- the defenses shown against guns are the same as those shown against sticks.

A few examples of kneeling and dagger and sword katas follow.

FRONT REACH KATA

442-447.   From the kneeling kata starting position, uke grabs cloth with both hands. Tori breaks the grip with an upward thrust of both arms and grips uke's left hand with his left hand. Placing his right hand at the back of uke's elbow, he twists uke's captured hand and applies an arm bar and inward wrist lock (photos 38-40, 24-26).

442

443

444

445

446

447

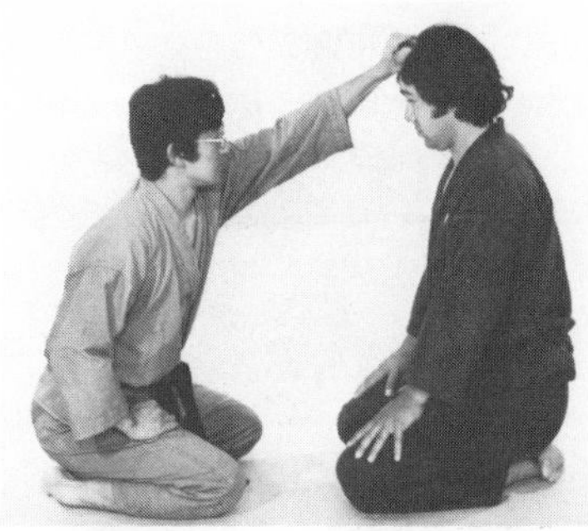

448

449

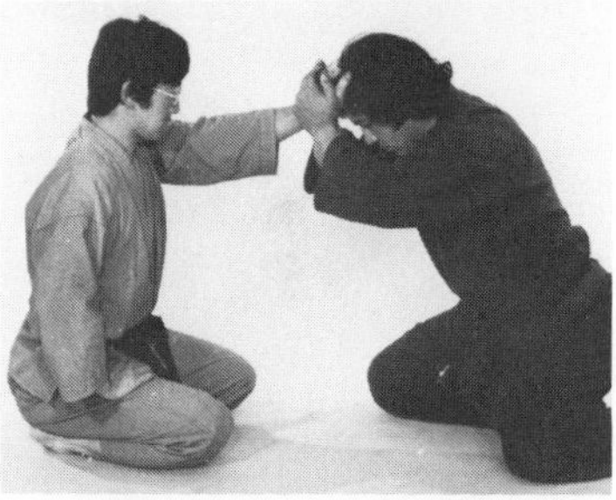

450

451

HAIR GRAB KATA

448.   From the standard starting position, uke grabs tori's hair.

449-451.   Tori places both of his hands on top of uke's hand, and pressing on the hand as he leans forward, tori applies a hand lock (photos 27, 28).

BACK CHOKE KATA

452.   From the starting position, uke slides around behind tori and chokes him.

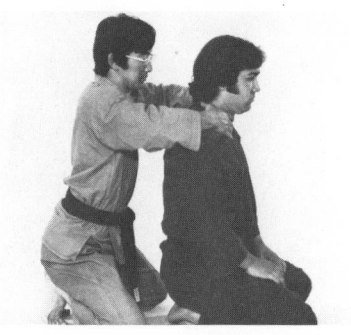

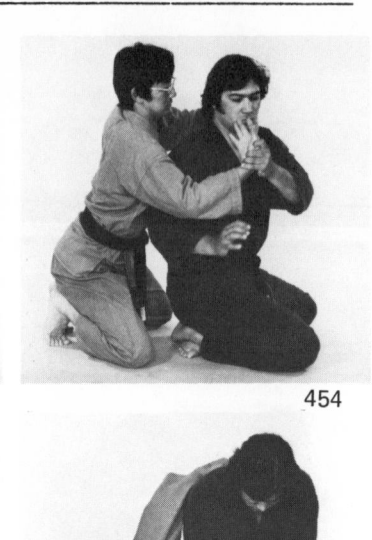

453

454

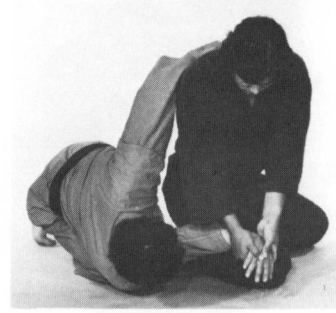

455   456

453.   Tori grips uke's right hand with his left hand...

454.   twists...

455.   and grips it with his right hand to apply an outward wrist lock (photos 20-23)...

456.   with follow-through pressure to take uke down.

457   458

FIST ATTACK KATA

457. From the starting position, uke slides around to kneel at tori's side.

458. Uke attempts a punching fist attack...

459. which tori stops by grabbing the fist with his left hand and gripping the elbow...

460. and he applies a bent-arm lever lock (photos 61-65).

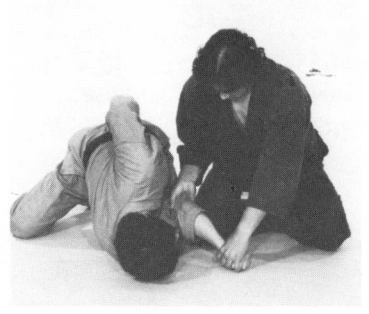

459

460

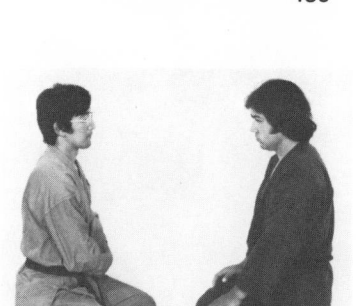

461

462

FRONT DAGGER ATTACK KATA

461. Tori kneels in the standard starting position; uke kneels with his arms crossed -- the dagger concealed in his sleeve.

462. Uke attacks. Tori grips the wrist with his right hand...

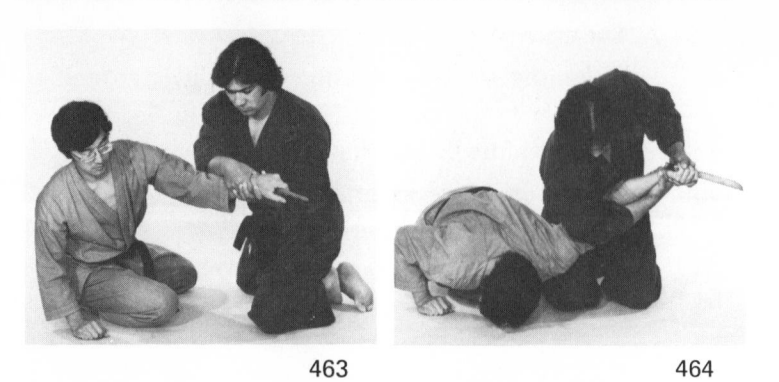

463   464

463. and twists it as he grips with his left hand and turns counterclockwise...

464. to apply an upper arm lock (photos 58-60).

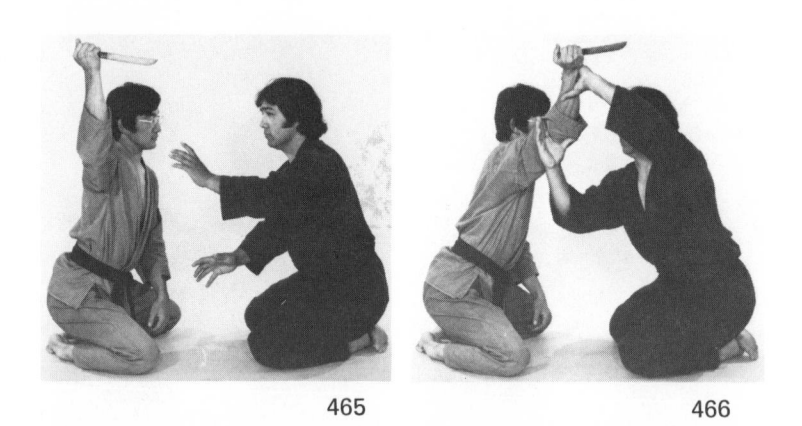

465   466

OVERHEAD DAGGER ATTACK KATA

465. Uke attacks with an overhead dagger thrust...

466. and tori grabs the wrist with his left hand as he grips the elbow with his right hand...

467. and twists the captured arm...

468. to apply a bent-arm lever lock (photos 61-65).

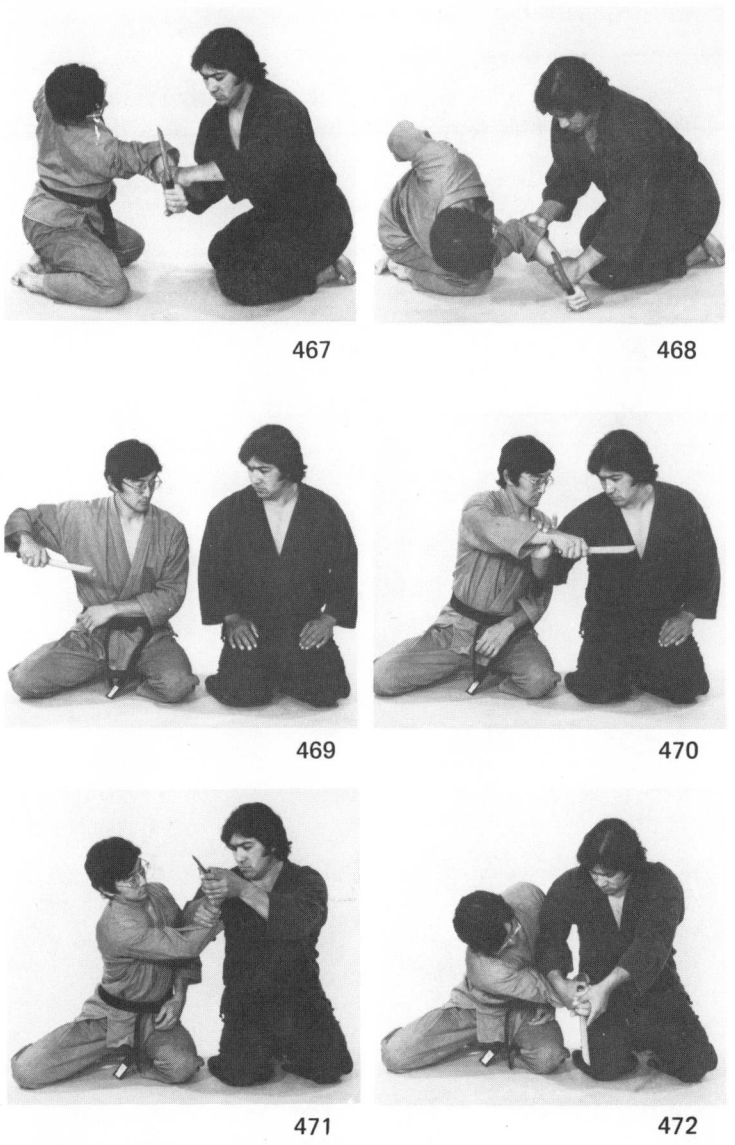

467

468

469

470

471

472

SIDE DAGGER ATTACK KATA

469-472.   Uke slides around to tori's side, draws his
dagger and thrusts. Tori grabs uke's wrist with his right
hand, twists and grips the hand with his left hand and
applies an outward wrist lock (photos 20-23).

STANDING SWORD ATTACK KATAS

Beginning Procedure

473.   Tori and uke stand facing each other; uke's un-sheathed sword is represented by a stick placed in his belt.

474.   Uke draws the sword and...

475.   begins the attack before tori makes any move.

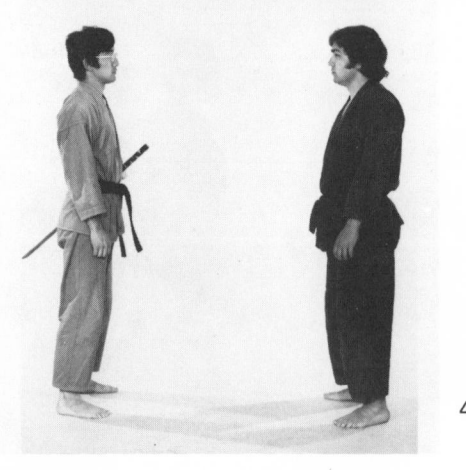

473

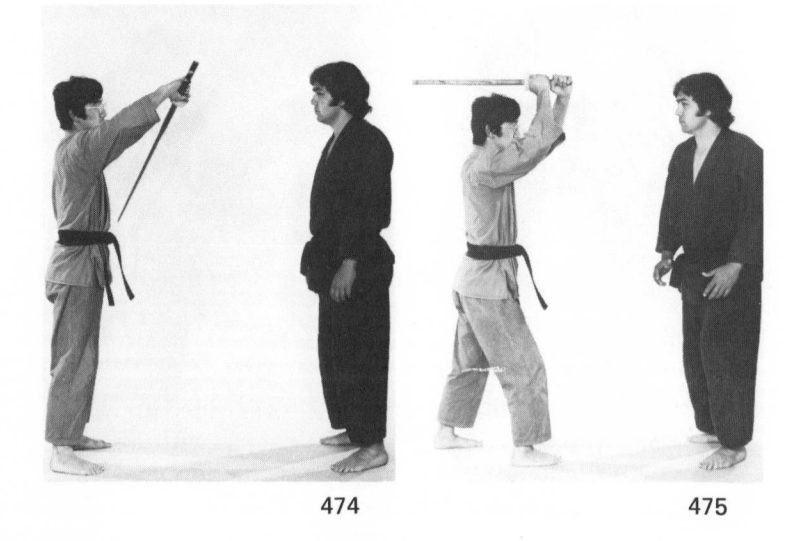

474   475

Overhead Sword Attack Kata

476-479. Uke attacks as in photo 475; tori parries with both hands. Tori grips uke's wrist with his right hand and pulls it as he wheels clockwise. Extending uke's arm across his chest, tori applies the hand and arm lever (photos 161-164).

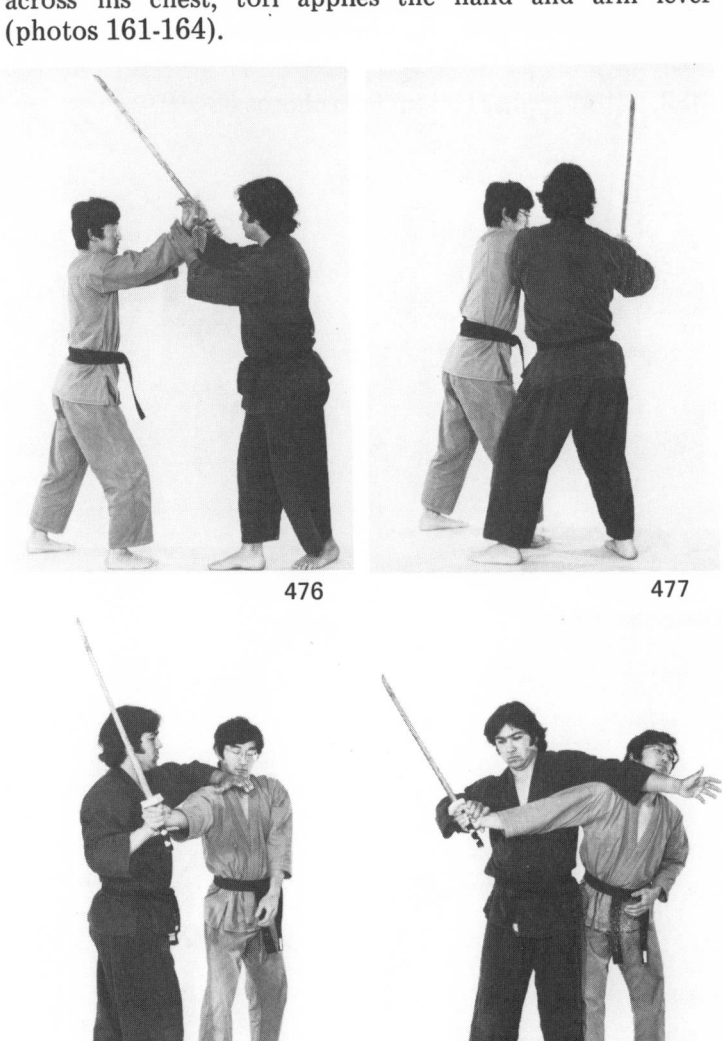

476

477

478

479

Forward Sword Attack Kata

480.   Uke draws his sword and begins a forward thrust...

481.   which tori parries by stepping to the outside of the thrusting sword and striking an open-hand blow with his left hand...

482.   and gripping and twisting the wrist with his right hand...

483.   tori applies an arm bar (photos 38-40).

480

481

482

483

BIBLIOGRAPHY

Collingridge, W. H. 1958. Tricks of Self-Defence. London: Thorsons Pub. Ltd.

Ferrara, V. P., Ed. 1942. Super Ju Jitsu. Chicago: Nelson-Hall Co.

Garrud, W. H. 1914. The Complete Jujitsuan. London: Methuen & Co. Ltd.

Hancock, H. I. & Higashi, K. 1961. The Complete Kano Jiu-Jitsu (Judo). New York: Dover Pub. Inc.

Hancock, H. I. 1905. Jiu-Jitsu Combat Tricks. New York and London: G. P. Putnam's Sons.

Harrison, E. J. No publishing date. The Fighting Spirit of Japan. London: W. Foulsham & Co. Ltd.

Kano, J. 1937. Judo (Jujutsu). Tokyo: Maruzeň Co. Ltd.

Kawaishi, M. No publishing date. My Method of Self-Defence. London: W. Foulsham & Co. Ltd.

Koyama, K. and Minami, A. 1933. Jiu Jitsu. New York: American Sports Pub. Co.

Krutwig, R. J. 1969. Ju-Jutsu Im Bild. Munich: Friedrich Bassermann Verlagsbuchhandlung.

Longhurst, P. No publishing date. Jiu-Jitsu. London: The Bazaar, Exchange & Mart Ltd.

Longhurst, P. No publishing date. Ju Jutsu and Judo. London: Frederick Warne & Co. Ltd.

Lord, H. No publishing date. Lightning Ju-Jitsu. New York: Padell Book Co.

Lowell, F. P. 1942. Jiu-Jitsu. New York: The Ronald Press Co.

Mitose, J. M. No publishing date. What is Self Defense? (Kenpo Jiu-Jitsu). Honolulu: No publisher's name.

Moynahan, J. M., Jr. 1961. A Guide to Judo, Ju Jitsu and Associated Arts. No city or publisher listed.

Nakae, K. 1958. Jiu Jitsu Complete. New York: Lyle Stuart.

Shomer, L. 1937. Police Jiu-Jitsu. New York: Padell Book Co.

Sigward, R. H. 1958. Modern Self Defense. New York: William C. Copp & Assoc.

Skinner, H. H. 1904. Jiu-Jitsu. New York: Japan Pub. Co.

Sutherland, W. B. No publishing date. Ju-Jitsu Self-Defence. London: Thomas Nelson and Sons Ltd.

Tomiki, K. 1956. Judo - Appendix: Aikido. Tokyo: Japan Travel Bureau.

Uyenishi, S. K. No publishing date. The Text-Book of Ju-Jutsu. London: Athletic Pub. Ltd.

Vairamuttu, R. A. No publishing date. Scientific Unarmed Combat. London: W. Foulsham & Co. Ltd.

Yabe, Y. K. 1904. A Course of Instruction in Jiu-Jitsu. No city listed: Clark, Dudley & Co.

Yoshida, J. 1934. Jiu-Jitsu Combat. Los Angeles: The American School of Jiu-Jitsu.

Yoshida, J. 1934. Secrets of Jiu-Jitsu. Los Angeles: The American School of Jiu-Jitsu.

ABOUT THE AUTHOR

BRUCE TEGNER is a specialist in sport and self-defense forms of weaponless fighting skills. He is regarded as this country's outstanding authority, teacher and innovator in the field.

He was born in Chicago, Illinois, in 1929. Both his parents were professional teachers of judo and jujitsu. They began to instruct him when he was two years old! Until he was eight, his mother and father trained him in fundamentals; after that he was taught by Asian and European experts. At the age of ten he began to teach -- assisting in the instruction of children's classes at his parents' school. At seventeen, he was the youngest second-degree (nidan) black belt on record in the United States.

In a field in which most individuals study only one specialty, Bruce Tegner's background is unusual. His education covered many aspects of weaponless fighting as well as stick and sword techniques. At the age of twenty-one, after he had become the California state judo champion, he gave up competition to devote himself fully to teaching, writing and teacher-training.

In the United States armed forces Mr. Tegner trained teachers to instruct weaponless combat, he taught military police tactics and he coached sport judo teams. He has trained actors and has devised fight scenes for films and television. From 1952 to 1967 he operated his own school in Hollywood where he taught men, women, children, exceptionally gifted students and blind and disabled persons.

Bruce Tegner has many books in print in this subject field. He has been highly praised in reviews by professionals in library and physical education journals and by psychologists. The books range from basic, practical self-defense to exotic forms of fighting for experts and enthusiasts. They are used as physical education texts, in recreation centers, by law enforcement training academies and by individuals throughout the world. Editions of Tegner titles have been published in French, German, Spanish, Portuguese and Dutch.

BRUCE TEGNER books are on sale at bookstores throughout the world. If your local dealer does not stock the titles you want, you may order directly from the publisher.

FOR A FREE LISTING of Bruce Tegner books on self-defense, judo, karate, kung fu, jujitsu and other specialties in the martial arts field and the inspirational books of *ELLEN KEI HUA* write:

THOR PUB. CO.
P O BOX 1782
VENTURA CA 93002